"Love is the song of the soul, singing to God."

Paramahansa Yogananda

SONGS OF THE SOUL

by

Paramahansa Yogananda

SELF-REALIZATION FELLOWSHIP
Founded by Paramahansa Yogananda
Sri Daya Mata, President
1983

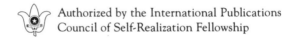 Authorized by the International Publications Council of Self-Realization Fellowship

Self-Realization Fellowship was founded in 1920 by Paramahansa Yogananda to be the instrument for the worldwide dissemination of his teachings. The reader can be certain of the authenticity of writings and recordings by or about Paramahansa Yogananda and his teachings if the registered Self-Realization emblem, and/or the statement of authorization (shown together above), appears on that work.

Library of Congress Catalog Number: 83-60701
ISBN 0-87612-025-7

Printed in the United States of America

10269-54321

PUBLISHER'S NOTE

It is with deep satisfaction that we offer this treasury of poems by Paramahansa Yogananda. The present volume fulfills a long-standing desire to restore to print those poems of his that were published in earlier years under the title *Songs of the Soul,* and to bring together under that title many of Paramahansaji's other poems from various Self-Realization publications, past and present.

Considerable thought and research have gone into the preparation of this edition. Original writings and transcripts were compared with variant renderings introduced by early editors, and by Paramahansaji himself; for he would sometimes pen corrections and creative variations that came to him when rereading a poem, or interpolate a fresh inspiration while reciting a passage in the course of a lecture or devotional service. The number of such variations in a poem is generally proportionate to the frequency of its use. In many cases they are slight — a more precise word, a different turn of phrase, occasionally a deletion (or addition) of a thought, or of certain lines, to fit a particular context. The present endeavor has been to adhere to Paramahansaji's original handwritten or spoken version; and from the modifications he introduced, to retain those that substantially clarify his thought or otherwise add to the beautiful imagery of his inspiration.

We were happy to find and restore not only illustrative words and phrases, but also entire lines or stanzas that had been omitted from these poems when they were originally published. The following are a few examples:

In the selection, *Flower Offering,* some of the phrases omitted or changed in the first version printed in 1923, and now restored in this new edition are

devotion-sweetened musk

("devotion-sweetened musk" instead of "devotion's perfume")

with silent song in me
I come to worship Thee

("With silent song in me" — this line was omitted — "I come to worship Thee")

An entire new stanza has been added. Written in rough draft by Paramahansaji, but never printed:

For naught from Thee I prayor long
That I bring offering song
I want just to tell
In secret what I feel

("For naught from Thee I pray or long
That I bring offering and song.
I just want to tell
In secret what I feel.")

In *Thy Homecoming,* "the steady sentinels" was misread and printed originally as "speedy sentinels":

the steady sentinels of sun & moon

of are patiently waiting for Thy home-coming.

("The steady sentinels of sun and moon are patiently
waiting for Thy homecoming").

In *A Mirror New,* the word "loyal" had been omitted:

would loyal show, all true

("Would loyal show, all true").

The charming line,

Ere the Sorcerer sleep doth call

("Ere the sorcerer Sleep doth call"),
had also been left out.

In *At the Roots of Eternity,* several unused descriptive
words and phrases from the original handwritten copy were
restored, such as:

with singing leaves

("with singing leaves," instead of "swaying trees")

with bounding planet-balls

("with bounding planet-balls," instead of "whirling
planets")

nectar loot

("nectar loot," which had not been included).

In *Listen to My Soul Song,* possibly the editor could not make out the handwritten word "gloaming,"

Beneath the gloaming of dim devotion of eyes unseeing

("Beneath the gloaming of dim devotion of eyes
unseeing").

It was originally printed as "gloom of dim devotion." That first printing also omitted the phrase "of eyes unseeing."

Similar corrections and restorations were made in many of the other poems as well, such as the addition in *Variety* of two previously unpublished stanzas at the end, and the picturesque phrase

Thy debut O Eternity

("Thy debut, O Eternity").

With this scanning of original manuscripts and transcriptions, we feel we have accomplished the review of these poems that Paramahansaji had started, but did not have time to finish. Since in many cases there was more than one "original" or "approved" version, we have chosen for this edition the rendering most often recited by Paramahansaji himself. Where such evidence was lacking, we selected those words or phrases deemed most characteristic of his unique mode of expression — as cited in the foregoing examples.

Songs of the Soul is an outpouring of Paramahansa Yogananda's direct perceptions of God—God in nature, in man, in everyday experiences, and in the spiritually awakened state of *samadhi* meditation. Most of the poems were written during the 1920s and 1930s. This was a period when Paramahansaji was traveling extensively throughout the United States to lecture in her principal cities. He wrote about what he saw, and about the inner experiences evoked by those perceptions. His writings are not the considered renderings of a poet's fancies, but a revelation of the interior experiences of a soul ever awake in God, responding to the wonders of nature; to the memories of a beloved motherland; to the deep impressions made by new friends and acquaintances; above all, to the divine realizations born of that soul's intimate communion with God.

SELF-REALIZATION FELLOWSHIP

Los Angeles, California
July 1983

AIMS AND IDEALS

of

Self-Realization Fellowship

As set forth by Paramahansa Yogananda, Founder

Sri Daya Mata, President

To disseminate among the nations a knowledge of definite scientific techniques for attaining direct personal experience of God.

To teach that the purpose of life is the evolution, through self-effort, of man's limited mortal consciousness into God Consciousness; and to this end to establish Self-Realization Fellowship temples for God-communion throughout the world, and to encourage the establishment of individual temples of God in the homes and in the hearts of men.

To reveal the complete harmony and basic oneness of original Christianity as taught by Jesus Christ and original Yoga as taught by Bhagavan Krishna; and to show that these principles of truth are the common scientific foundation of all true religions.

To point out the one divine highway to which all paths of true religious beliefs eventually lead: the highway of daily, scientific, devotional meditation on God.

To liberate man from his threefold suffering: physical disease, mental inharmonies, and spiritual ignorance.

To encourage "plain living and high thinking"; and to spread a spirit of brotherhood among all peoples by teaching the eternal basis of their unity: kinship with God.

To demonstrate the superiority of mind over body, of soul over mind.

To overcome evil by good, sorrow by joy, cruelty by kindness, ignorance by wisdom.

To unite science and religion through realization of the unity of their underlying principles.

To advocate cultural and spiritual understanding between East and West, and the exchange of their finest distinctive features.

To serve mankind as one's larger Self.

CONTENTS

Alphabetical List of Poems by Title

Photographs Associated
With the Life of Paramahansa Yogananda

Dedicated
to my earthly father,
who has helped me in all my spiritual
work in India and America

CONSECRATION

At Thy feet I come to shower
All my full heart's rhyming flower:
Of Thy breath born,
By Thy love grown,
Through my lonely seeking found,
By hands Thou gavest plucked and bound.

For Thee, the sheaves
Within these leaves:
The choicest flowers
Of my life's season,
With petals soulful spread,
Their humble perfume shed.

Hands folded, I come now to give
What's Thine. Receive!

THE GARDEN OF THE NEW YEAR

The echoes of last year, its sorrow and laughter,
Have died away.
The song-voice of the New Year — encouraging,
    hope-imparting—
Is chanting:
"Refashion life ideally!"

Abandon the weeds of old worries.
From the forsaken garden of the past
Garner only seeds of joys and achievements,
Hopes, good actions and thoughts, all noble
    desires.

Sow in the fresh soil of each new day
Those valiant seeds; water and tend them
Until your life is fragrant
With rare flowering qualities.

The New Year whispers:
"Awaken your habit-dulled spirit
To zestful new effort.
Rest not till th' eternal freedom is won
And ever-pursuing karma outwitted!"

With joy-enlivened, unendingly united mind
Let us all dance forward, hand in hand,
To reach the Halcyon Home
Whence we shall wander no more.

MY SOUL IS MARCHING ON

*Never be discouraged by this motion picture of life. Salvation
is for all. Just remember that no matter what happens to you,
still your soul is marching on. No matter where you go, your
wandering footsteps will lead you back to God. There is no
other way to go.*

The shining stars are sunk in darkness deep,
The weary sun is dead at night,
The moon's soft smile doth fade anon;
But still my soul is marching on!

The grinding wheel of time hath crushed
Full many a life of moon and star,
And many a brightly smiling morn;
But still my soul is marching on!

The flowers bloomed, then hid in gloom,
The bounty of the trees did cease;
Colossal men have come and gone,
But still my soul is marching on!

The aeons one by one are flying,
My arrows one by one are gone;
Dimly, slowly, life is fading,
But still my soul is marching on!

Darkness, death, and failures vied;
To block my path they fiercely tried.
My fight with jealous Nature's strong,
But still my soul is marching on!

WHEN WILL HE COME?

When every heart's desire pales
Before the brilliancy of the ever-leaping flames
   of God-love,
Then He will come.

When, in expectation of His coming,
You are ever ready
To fearlessly, grieflessly, joyously
Burn the faggots of all desires
In the fireplace of life,
That you may protect Him from your freezing
   inner indifference,
Then He will come.

When no inclinations or unfulfilled cravings
Can be sure of your stability toward them;
When He shall be certain you will never leave
   the guru,
Then He will come.

No matter how you feel — helpless, forsaken,
Tortured by temptation, karma, or tests —
If you ever keep hoping He will come,
He will come.

When your mind says piercingly,
"You can't have Him, you don't deserve

having Him";
Still, if your soul, disregarding all this,
Shall ever keep chanting within, "He will come,"
He will come.

When He shall be sure nothing else can claim you,
Then He will come.

Even if you are the sinner of sinners,
Still, if you never stop calling Him deeply
In the temple of unceasing love,
Then He will come.

VANISHING BUBBLES

Many unknown bubbles float and flow,
Many ripples dance by me
And melt away into the sea;
I yearn to know, ah, whence they come
    and whither go.

The rain drops and dies,
My thoughts play wild and vanish quick,
The red clouds melt into the skies;
I stake my purse, I'll slave all life, their motive
    still to seek.

Some friends — though not their love —
Some dearest thoughts I ne'er would lose, I said;
And last night's surest stars, seen just above,
All, all are fled.

Crowds of lilies, warbling linnets,
Perfumed blossoms, honey-mad bees
Once met at yonder bowered trees;
But now the lonesome field alone is left.

The bubbles, lilies, friends, dramatic thoughts,
Their parts did play, and entertain;
And now behind the cosmic screen,
Their displayed coats to change,
They quiet, concealed, remain.

THE SCREEN OF LIFE

When dawn breaks the spell of darkness,
And roses bloom;
When little pleasures all dance round you,
And fickle festivity sings
Of babes newborn (in future sure to die);
When fortune laughs
And praise weaves garlands
And glory makes the crown;
When on all sides men shout your praises
And thousands follow —
You see His hands showering blessings.

Yet in the limbs of the rosebush, leafless o'er
    the snow,
There is a silent budding joy in every twig.
There is a joy in waiting
For the streak of dawn in the dark;
Through vapors of sorrow dim, joy is seen with
    welcome.

Persecution sweetens oft-tasted praise;
A bare head expectant of the crown
Has joy denied the head long diademed.
In the uncertain darkness, each little flame of joy
    burns brighter;
The mine of monotony holds the caged air
    of bursting gaiety.

Old age thrills with the thought of youth;
Behind the veil of death hides the promise
    of new birth.

The shifting scenes of life screen the true Life:
Behind the unreal motion pictures of things seen
Unfolds the real drama
Of stable Cosmic Life unseen.
Shadows are lined with light,
Sorrows bulge with joy,
Failures are potent with determination for success,
Cruelties urge the instinct to be kind.

Passing mirth, fame, wealth,
Proud possessions (giv'n only to be taken away),
And the straw fires of passions, pleasures,
    and intoxicating friendships
Oft do hide His presence;
But when all are gone, you look for Him.
In that solitude, by friends and foes avoided,
There's One unseen, who ne'er forsakes.
Though He may fly when all are shaking hands
    with you,
When none stand by, He comes to take your hand.

SHADOWS

Beds of flowers, or vales of tears;
Dewdrops on buds of roses,
Or miser souls, as dry as desert sands;
The little running joys of childhood,
Or the stampede of wild passions;
The ebbing and rising of laughter,
Or the haunting melancholy of sorrow;
The will-o'-the-wisp of our desire,
Leading only from mire to mire;
The octopus grip of self-complacency
And time-beaten habits;
The first cry of the newborn babe,
And the last groan of death;
The bursting joy of health,
Or the ravages of cruel disease —
These, all these, but shadows are,
Seen by us on the cosmic mental screen.
Shadows, and nothing but shadows!
Yet shadows have, oh, so many shades —
Dark ones, light ones —
So even shadows may entertain.

ONE THAT'S EVERYWHERE

The wind plays,
The tree sighs,
The sun smiles,
The river moves.
Feigning dread, the sky is blushing red
At the sun-god's gentle tread.
Earth changes robes
Of black and starlit night
For dazzling golden light.

Dame Nature loves herself t'array
In changing seasons' colors gay.
The murmuring brook e'er tries to tell
In lisping sounds so well
Of the hidden thought
By inner spirit brought.
The birds aspire to sing
Of things unknown that swell within.
But man first speaks in language true—
Both loud and clear, with meaning new—
Of That all else before
Had failed to full declare,
Of One that's everywhere.

WHERE I AM

Not the lordly domes on high
With tall heads daring clouds and sky,
Nor shining alabaster floors,
Nor the rich organ's awesome roar,
Nor rainbowed windows' beauty quaint—
Colossal chronicles told in paint—
Nor torch nor incense' curling soar,
Nor pure-dressed children of the choir,
Nor well-planned sermon,
Nor loud-tongued prayer
Can call Me there.
The richly carven door,
Through which vain pomp and pride have poured
I deign not through to go;
But still, I come — incognito.
The stony, polished altar grand
And narrow-builded sermon seat,
Too cramped, they seem, to hold
My large, large body for retreat.

A humble magnet call,
A whisper by the brook,
On grassy altar small—
There I have My nook.
A crumbling temple shrine,
A little place unseen,
Unhedged, unwatched,

Is where I humbly rest and lean.*

A sacred heart
Tear-washed and true
Doth draw Me with its rue.
I take no bribe—
Of strength or wealth,
Of caste or church or scribe,
Of fame or faith or festive breath—
But wail for truth.
And e'er the distant broken heart
Doth draw Me, e'en to heathen lands:
And My help in silence I impart.

* "Lean" should be read in the sense of "prefer."

IN STILLNESS DARK

Hark!
In stillness dark—
When noisy dreams have slept,
The house has gone to rest
And busy life
Doth cease its strife—
The soul in pity soft doth kiss
The truant flesh, to soothe,
And speaks with mind-transcending grace
In soundless voice of peace.

Through transient fissures deep
In walls of sleep,
Take thou a gentle peep.
Droop not, nor stare,
But watch with care
The sacred glare,*
Ablaze and clear,
In blissful golden glee
Flash past thee
So nigh.
Ashamed, Apollo droops in dread
To see that luster overspread
The boundless reach of inner sky.

* The light of the spiritual eye, seen in deep meditation.

17

SILENCE

The earth, the planets, play
In and through the sun-born rays
In majesty profound.
> Umpire Time
> In silence sublime
> Doth watch
> This cosmic match.

The Author of the wondrous game
Assumes no spoken name.
With boundless poise
He doth His will, without a noise;
> Ungrateful moods ignoring,
> Unkindness all forgiving.

Truth clearly speaks to all,
> But speaks not loud.
> They hear its call
> Who noise enthrall.*
The voice in threatening silence speaks
To each who error's pathway seeks.

---

* I.e., those who practice yoga techniques of meditation, which enable the mind to disconnnect itself from sensory distractions, thus freeing it to experience perceptions of the Indwelling Glory.

The tiger may be tamed,
Failure's talons can be maimed,
All friends forsaking reason's way regained,
Unruly nature trained,
By powerful silence of unspoken words,
If in truth maintained.

.

THE NOBLE NEW

Sing songs that none have sung,
Think thoughts that ne'er in brain have rung,
Walk in paths that none have trod,
Weep tears as none have shed for God,
Give peace to all to whom none other gave,
Claim him your own who's everywhere disclaimed.
Love all with love that none have felt, and brave
The battle of life with strength unchained.

WAKE, WAKE, MY SLEEPING
HUNGER, WAKE!

When tables large — of earth and moon and
    meteors,
Of brooks and rills, of shining ether ore —
Are laid with wondrous One Nectar,
Stolen from nature's nooks by lares,
Do thou thy sullen sleep forsake:
Wake, wake, my sleeping Hunger, wake!

Through diverse paths of aeons thou hast cried
For a morsel of manna; thou hast begged and tried.
But now thou sleepest, dazed and tired;
On cheeks undried lie drops
Of fresh-wept tears
While Nectar touches thy lips — partake!
Wake, wake, my sleeping Hunger, wake!

This unquenched Hunger old of mine
Did eat all fare, and yet did pine —
Was starved with surfeit, and it sought
How might its yearned-for food be got.
The food for which thou wept'st awaits — partake!
Wake, wake, my sleeping Hunger, wake!

Friends, wealth, and fancy's rarest treat,
Posthumous wishes sprung from deathless roots
    so sweet,

And burned with thousand flaming waves,
Did fail to quell thy heart's true crave.
The Nectar sought for seeks thee now — partake!
Wake, wake, my sleeping Hunger, wake!

My Hunger, thou hast burned and wept to drink
Life's mysteries by life's bare brink —
Ambrosial founts that sleep beneath
Sequestered caves in soil of truth.
Oh, weep more drops, nay, streams — oceans
    of tears.
Thy duty is for peace to weep; thine only care
To seek thy work; and all thy food
Be what doth feed thy mood.
Thy work is done; thy Nectar's here —
Quench, quench th' eternal ache!
Wake, wake, my sleeping Hunger, wake!

FREEDOM

Brave cords, bind me hand and foot;
Yet lo, I am free, ever free.
Disease, ply your tortures;
Still I am free, ever free.
Health, try your lures;
But see, I am free, ever free.
Death, destroy if you will
My body-prison; caged or uncaged,
I am free, ever free.

Forged in the furnace of incarnations,
Long chains of earthly desires
Have tried to bind me;
But I escaped from life to life,
And at last I am free, ever free.
Through the portal of the rainbow
I entered heaven's free skies;
Now I am free, ever free.

Naught can bind me
If I bind not myself.
None can free me
If I know not I am free.
Knowing that naught exists to bind me,
I know I am free, ever free.

AFTER THIS

After the prison-petals of earth-life fade,
And the soul-scent slips
Into the mighty cosmic wind of Spirit,
No more would I love a flower-cage life—
Unless to mingle the dewdrop tears of other
 prisoned souls with mine,
And show them the way that I my freedom won.

Oh, I would not mind dwelling
In roses and daffodils, for a time,
If it is of my own free will;
But *forever* to stay behind bars of beauty
Of violet-sun-gold rays, I care not.
No more will I be compelled to live
Even in a golden heavenly cage.

From flower to flower will I fly.
I will wear the blackness of the night,
Shimmering with busy stars—
I will be the twinkle of their lights.
I will be the waking of the dawn,
And burst forth with the warming rays
 of friendship.
I will be the shepherd of stray souls,
Or the humblest lamb in all His fold;
The most famous man,
Or the least known of a cycle.

I will be the tiniest cosmic spark;
Or roll as the mighty vapors of life,
Dashing my power-fed soul
Against the rocks of worldly strife.
I will be the clouds, donning rainbow garlands.
I will puff bubbles of planets with my breath,
And float them on the waves of space.
I will be the babble of the brook,
And the voice of the nightingale.

As emotion-waves, I will surge in the sea of souls.
Holding to the log of laughter,
I will float to the shores of bliss.
I will sing through the voices of all;
I will preach through all temples and prayers.
I will love with the love of God.
I will think with the thoughts of all;
The hearts of all will be my heart;
The souls of all will be my soul;
And the smiles of all, my smile.

FOUNTAIN OF SMILES

Bestow not sarcastic smiles
Born from the dark womb of hate.
Welcome not bandit smiles,
Which rob thy trueness.
Wear not serpent smiles,
Which hide their venom
Behind a sting of laughter.
Banish volcanic smiles
Of subterranean wrath.
Bedim not the mirror of soul — thy face —
With shades of pitying smiles.
Let no witless, noisy, muscle-contorting laughs,
Like rowdies, echo an emptiness of thy soul.

A fountain of joy
Must gush from the soil of thy mind
To spread in all directions
Fine sprays of smiles,
Like vital veins
Running through laugh-thirsty hearts.
Let the lake of thy smiles break its embankment
And spread to territories of Infinitude.
Let thy smiles
Rush through lonely stars
To brighten their twinkles.

The flood of thy laughter

Will inundate the drought of dry minds,
Sweeping away the barriers of cold formalities.
Spread thy smile like the dawn
To vanish the gloom of minds.
Paint thy golden smiles on every dark spot,
Brightening cloudy days.
Command thy smiles to resurrect life
In the walking dead.
Smile for the dead,
For their grim peace bespeaks their victory
    o'er pain.
Let thy smiles
Pulverize to atoms the rocks of sorrow.
Let thy smiles meander
Through desert-souls and oasis-hearts alike.
Let the deluge of thy fearless smiles
Sweep through all minds and every place,
Drowning, washing away
All barriers for miles and miles.

When God laughs through the soul,
And the soul beams through the heart,
And the heart smiles through the eyes,
Then the Prince of Smiles
Is enthroned beneath the canopy
Of thy celestial brow.
Protect thy Prince of Smiles in the castle of
    sincerity.
Let no rebel hypocrisy lurk to destroy it.

Spread the gospel of "Smile!"
Purify all homes with thy healthy smiles.

Let loose the wildfire of thy smiles,
And blaze the thickets of melancholia.
Open the long-bottled-up musk of smiles,
Releasing its perfume to waft in all directions.
Intoxicate all with the wine of thy smiles.
Take the rich gifts of smiles from every
    joyous soul,
And from the Mine of all true mirth.
Then north, south, east, west, where'er thou goest,
Thou smile millionaire,
Scatter thy golden smiles
Freely, freely, everywhere.

THE HUMAN MIND

I love to roam alone, unseen,
In cities of the human mind.
I prize the streets untrod by crooked thoughts—
Vile-born, unkind.

Incognito I wish to wander—
To living lanes my thoughts surrender—
With simple wish to know and learn
Each straight and righteous path and danger-turn.

I wish to roam in mazy lanes
Of dark and brighter thoughts;
With love to all and harm to none,
With better message fraught.

I'd like to broaden narrow lanes
Of selfish, twisted thought
With my love's true-building brain—
Soul's wisdom — that I've within me got.

I long to soar so high,
That I at once may spy
The narrow alleys and broader roads
Of thoughtful human moods.

PAUPACK'S PEAK

O Paupack's Peak,
'Mid rustic scenes and trees
I found thee; and did seek
In thee the Hidden Beauty.

Thy palace I approached by woodsy road;
Where on both sides there stood
Thy columned trees, with leafy swords outstretched
To render bowered welcome.

Unconscious hopes did thrill
To know thy mysteries royal;
And tempted was I
Thy secrets to pry.

I stole through secret hilly ways — and all at once
Stood face to face
With beauteous scene
Where liquid silver spray did grace
The breast of caves; and down did run,
Sparkling through rays of sun
To ornament crude stones and logs beneath
With eddying necklaces
And pearly bubbled wreaths.

I tore through veil of trees — all sudden spied
Thy peaceful Paupack, and in wonder cried

To find on cloudy breast of proud high hills
A lake,
Of myriad tears close-gathered — mirror still —
Full ready to be kind and slake
The thirst of my parched mind
The Unseen Strength to find.

Cool breezes wooed the warm lake waters,
Half-hidden in a snow-white mist
That did not resist
Invasion of two leaflike canoe vessels —
Gliding like peaceful swans
At farewell hour of the sun.
In mind's swift-passing fantasy,
Like mystic barks they seemed,
Laden with silhouetted singing angels
Sailing across the sky.

I entered once a covered path,
Inlaid with velvet moss
And sunshine-checkered leafy cushion.
Their silken forms the leaves did give for
    all to tread
And dance in comfort on their wavy bed.
Could wealth audacious ever dare to make
Such bowered garland, never fading, for a lake —
Of countless rhododendrons, white and pink,
Whose flowers are each summer born,
The woodland darkness to adorn?

I passed through corridors of trees
That tried to hide with finger-leaves
The lake's pure sparkling beauty on my left.
Of cares bereft,
I walked the garland path
And many a time, in wrath
Did I command my noisy footsteps and my thoughts:
"In stillness stand!"
And then I bowed, in sweetest reverence,
To the Spirit in this temple of silence.

As motionless I stood, and gazed within, without—
At thoughts and feelings, leaves and stones,
   my body, sky and earth and light—
Where'er I looked, whate'er I saw,
Thy tender Peeping Eyes
My soul did draw.

THY CALL

When lost I roam,
I hear Thy call to Home —
In whistling breeze,
In rustling leaves of trees.

When, drunk in folly,
I wander gaily
By the sandy shore,
Who wakes me with a sudden roar?

When clouds o'erspread their veil,
My precious joy to steal,
Who tears that shroud away
And bursts in redd'ning ray?

When dark night blinds
And movement binds,
Who shows my path and th' dark beguiles
With mildly mocking moonlit smiles?

The million starry stares,
The waking sunny glare,
Thy river's ever murm'ring air,
Thy sure and silent call declare.

FOR THEE AND THINE

I love to seek what's mine.
I think, I act,
I work with tact
To gain what's mine.

I pass by the river,
Aflow in joyous quiver,
To soothe this mind of mine.
I smell the flowers
To cheer the hours—
I love to have what's mine.

I sip the golden sunshine
To warm this flesh of mine.
I drink the fresh and flowing air;
For me I lift my prayer.
I try to rake
The world to take
All things for me and mine.

Those dark days are gone;
The old time's flown,
So lived for me and mine.
In new-born light
I see what's right:
To live for Thee and Thine.

'TIS ALL UNKNOWN

Each rosebud dawning day,
In hourly opening petal-rays,
Doth fair display
Its hidden beauty.
The petal-hours, unfolding smile,
My drooping, lagging heart beguile.
Day spreads its petals all
Of novel hopes and joys withal.
"Today" is here.

A rosebud's there!
In time the rosebud blooms,
While lazy day oft glooms.
Forsake thy sleep,
O lazy day!
Open thou with full-bloom ray
To chase my gathered gloom away!

The rosebud opened,
The day now smiled
In fullness fine.
Still I opine
'Tis all unknown
Just why the rose was blown;
And day was drowned in night,
Then raised again to light
Of glorious dawn,
So swiftly marching o'er the lawn!

PROTECTING THORNS

The charm of the blushing rose
Hides stinging thorns beneath.
Without some wounds from those,
Thou canst not snatch her wealth
E'en with stealth:
The rose that sprang from earthly sod,
Unplucked, with thorns unstained with blood.

In her defense the barbs do sting,
To keep thee out with thorny ring;
But perfumed petals' beguiling show
Thy drowsing soul doth wake and draw.
If thou dost love her beauty alone,
Why would'st thou rush
To bleed from prickly thorn?

BLOOD OF THE ROSE

I tore the rose,
I bled its slender stem;
Its petals quivered
And I shivered;
Yet dared to rob it of its smell!
My heart did break, and tell,
"Thy hands are soiled" — and mute I stood,
Thus self-condemned and stained with rose's blood.

But I know now,
I love the rose
More than its wealth, and vow
Ne'er its love to desecrate or lose.

UNDYING BEAUTY

They did their best
And they are blest —
The sap, the shoots,
The little leaves and roots;
The benign breath,
The touch of light —
All worked in amity
To grow the rose's beauty.
Watch its splendor,
Its undying grandeur,
The Infinite Face
That peeps through its little case.
Watch not in grief
Its falling petals or its brief
Sojourn here;
For its career
Done, its duty ends;
Toward the Immortal's home it tends.
The sap dried,
The summer petals fled,
Its body pines;
Yet its death's divine;
Through the death it spurns
Its deathless glory's won;
The rose is dead —
Its beauty lives instead.

MAKE US THYSELF

That forced silence on my last day will be a mystery
   sleep; my beautiful and nightmare dreams of
   earthly being will bid farewell — for a time, at
   least.
On the downy bed of blissful oblivion, a short rest;
   then I shall awake, on a new star, perchance, or
   in a new earthly setting — another dream of
   another life.
Maybe I shall be deluded still, thinking I am awake
   while yet I dream.

Will this sleeping and deluded waking in dreams
   continue until I know I can really awaken only in
   Thee?
Why hast Thou monopolized in Thyself the only
   wakefulness?
Why hast Thou kept hidden in Thy hands the only
   key to the mystery chamber of life and the
   hereafter?

If Thou art awake, why dost Thou want us to dream
   this cosmos?
Or art Thou also sleeping, dreaming that we are
   playing on the glittering, planet-studded stage of
   time?
Then in truth we are waking and dreaming within
   Thy dream.

Is it when Thou dost awake, dreaming no more,
   that we too shall cease to dream life and death,
   and stop our playing? Will all trees, all bodies,
   all bodiless souls then become Thyself?

In dreaming, we divide our minds into thoughts of
   many things — minds, mountains, souls, sky,
   stars—creating each "reality" out of the tissue of
   fancy. So hast Thou transformed Thy dreaming
   mind into the star-chequered savanna of the
   blue, with its indwelling planetary families, our
   earth — and us, sorrowing, laughing, coming,
   dying.
Thou canst be forgiven all the horrors of this
   cosmic drama only if it is a dream.
Even so, that which is dream-play to Thee is to us
   an awesome dream-struggle and death.

Since we and all things created are made of Thy
   dreaming mind, why dost Thou not wake up and
   dissolve us into Thy fearless, blessed Being?
Melt our dreaming minds into Thy mind, our
   temporary joys into Thine everlasting Joy.
Unite our fading life with Thine imperishable Life.
Blend our flickering, stale happiness into Thine
   enduring ever-new Blessedness.
Make us fearless, by letting us know that we are
   waking and dreaming in Thee; that we are Thine
   all-protected, ever-blissful Self.

THY DIVINE GYPSY

I will be a gypsy—
Roam, roam, and roam.
I will sing a song that none has sung!
I will sing to the sky,
I will sing to the winds,
I'll sing to my red clouds!
I'll roam, roam, and roam—
King of the lands through which I roam.

By day, the shady trees will be my tent.
At night, the stars will be
My candles, twinkling in the firmament;
And I will call the moon to be my lamp
And light my silver, skyey camp.
I will be a gypsy—
Roam, roam, and roam.

I will eat the food that chance may bring;
I will drink from crystal sparkling spring;
I will doff my cap and off will go.
Like a wayward brook of long ago,
I will roll o'er the green
And scatter the joy of all my heart
To birds, leaves, winds, hills — then depart
To stranger and stranger lands, from East to West.
Oh! I will be a gypsy—
Roam, roam, and roam!

But always, when I lay me down to rest,
I'll sing to Thee my gypsy prayer,
And find Thee, always, everywhere.

Oh, I will be Thy gypsy;
I'll roam and roam — through aeons roam.
But when 'tis time my soul to rest,
I'll dream of Thee whom I love best
And wake from many lifetimes' dreams fore'er.
Then Thou and I, as one, shall gypsy everywhere.

THOU AND I ARE ONE

Thy Cosmic Life and I are one.
Thou art the Spirit, and I am all nature;
 We are one.
Thou art the Ocean, and I am the wave;
 We are one.
Thou art the Ocean, and I am the drop;
 We are one.
Thou art the Flame, and I am the spark;
 We are one.
Thou art the Flower, and I am the fragrance;
 We are one.
Thou art the Song, and I am the music;
 We are one.

Thou art the Father, and I am Thy child;
 We are one.
Thou art my Mother, and I am Thy son;
 We are one.
Thou art my Friend, I am Thy friend;
 We are one.
Thou art the Beloved, and I am the lover;
 We are one.
Thou art the Lover, and I am the beloved;
 We are one.
Thou art the Master, and I am Thy servant;
 We are one.
Thou art my Guru, I am Thy disciple;

We are one.
Thou art all Laughter, I am a smile;
    We are one.
Thou art the Light, and I am the atom;
    We are one.
Thou art Consciousness, I am the thought;
    We are one.
Thou art Eternal Power, and I am strength;
    We are one.

Thy Peace and I are one.
Thy Joy and I are one.
Thy Wisdom and I are one.
Thy Love and I are one.
That is why Thou and I are one.
Thou and I were one, and Thou and I will be one
    evermore.

I WAS MADE FOR THEE

I was made for Thee alone. I was made for dropping
flowers of devotion gently at Thy feet on the altar
of the morning.

My hands were made to serve Thee willingly; to
remain folded in adoration, waiting for Thy
coming; and when Thou comest, to bathe Thy
feet with my tears.

My voice was made to sing Thy glory.

My feet were made to seek Thy temples everywhere.

My eyes were made a chalice to hold Thy burning
love and the wisdom falling from Thy nature's
hands.

My ears were made to catch the music of Thy
footsteps echoing through the halls of space, and
to hear Thy divine melodies flowing through all
heart-tracts of devotion.

My lips were made to breathe forth Thy praises and
Thine intoxicating inspirations.

My love was made to throw incandescent
searchlight flames to find Thee,

hidden in the forest of my desires.

My heart was made to respond to Thy call alone.

My soul was made to be the channel through which
Thy love might flow uninterruptedly into all
thirsty souls.

TATTERED GARMENT

Sing thou no plaintive lay
When my earthly raiment dies,
Nor let ashes tell thy tears where it lies.
Oh, blow my tattered garment's dust away!

Of dust clean-washed,
The hidden Gold beneath will show
Itself anew, all brightly brushed,
And shine somewhere with wisdom's glow.

It waits with luring luster
For the wandering Home-lorn soul —
To show the path, with lightning glimmer,
From darkness to the Goal.

WHAT USE?

Why did You give me eyes
If I cannot see You everywhere?
What use my hands
If they do not touch Your feet
Treading silently in the heart of all cosmic motions?
What use my feet
If they exert not to seek Your temple in every place?
What use my ears
If they do not with ecstatic attention
Hear the echo of Your voice in the soundless
    sermons of the scriptures?

What use my reason
If it does not lead me out of this cosmic conundrum
To the final home within You?
What use my will
If it wins everything but the freedom You bestow?
What use my feeling
If it thrills not to Your Presence in the lotus flowers
    of floating universes,
And in the electronic forget-me-nots
Glistening in the garden of time and space?
What use my love
If it feels not Your love secreted in all hearts—
Those that slumber in ignorance
And those prophetic ones that are awake in Thee?

FLOWER OFFERING

A goblet of my folly-blood
Is humbly set beneath Thy petaled feet,
   O Lotus Sweet!
I've stood with brimming cup of tears,
Seeking Thine angry thirst to quench.
With sandal sweet, and motley costumed flowers,
With devotion-sweetened musk from my heart
   of hearts,
With myrrh of age-old constancy my soul imparts,
With silent song in me,
I come to worship Thee.

Unheard, my mournful lay;
For naught, I cry and pray.
But still, with sleepless care,
I'll lay my flowers there.

Alternate closing stanza penned by the author:

For naught from Thee I pray or long
That I bring offerings and song.
I just want to tell
In secret what I feel,
And with watchful sleepless care
To lay my flowers here.

THE EVER NEW

Newer joys adorn the day;
Brighter burn, through livelong night,
The stars with purer light;
Wiser thoughts do brace my voice,
Unused words await my choice —
With heart of the new I'll sing my lay.

My wingèd thoughts do ceaseless beat
The sky of time, and race to meet
Thy Presence sweet, on distant throne,
Somewhere beyond the manifest, alone.

Each vernal day
Men chant their songs —
Not with thoughts the same, but changing throngs
Of newer ones that make Thy greater lay.

The bubbling joy
Of a little boy,
Each brew of friendship's still
I steal; and with them fill
Mine ageless cup of heart —
With ceaseless thrills 'twill start.

Morrow each, and each today
With unmatched love I'll sing my lay.
The voices same do choir their praise

In temple, church, and fane;
But I ne'er deign to hear
The strains all stained with age-old tear;
My fountain springs afresh today —
With tears ne'er shed before will flow my lay.

And in the same old church
I'll newly sing, and search
The same old sermon
For deeper truths and clearer reason;
And from the same old organ will I seek
Fresh notes of hope for the newborn week.

Every day, oh, every day
The bell will ring a new Sunday,
And bathèd in Thy beaming ray,
With newer thoughts I'll sing my lay.

CITY DRUM

'Tis morn. I hear
In rolling wheels the song
Of a marching world
So strong.

I love to be roused
From silent sleep
By the early hum
Of the active-city drum.

The drum doth beat
To loudly greet
All heroes true
That would die or do;
That meet the morning's foe
Of worry or of woe
With a dauntless smile,
And thus success beguile
Unto the happy camp
Where peace e'er burns its lamp.

With noisy hum
The city drum
Announces true and strong:
"The world is marching on."

SCENES WITHIN

Many a wondrous scenic face
Denver's horizon grand doth grace.
Yet when I think of the rarer beauties
That lie in human souls,
Rapture calls.

Eagerly I look;
Delving deep in valleys of human minds—
In all their sacred nooks.
Colossal mounts of nobility
I find, adorned with every goodly quality.

Marigolds, roses, pure white flowers
Of budding thoughts, their perfume wafting,
Attract me to their bowers.
The blue expanse of amity
Ripples with thrills of endless beauty.
From compassion's mountain-bosom,
Perpetual soul freshness, constant kind looks,
Flow down like brooks.
Founts of matchless love
Bubble forth in the heart
Of this soul-garden, and start
Endless sparkling fancies.

Yet in the land of souls
Blow various breezes;

One warms me, and another freezes.
Pure souls, vital souls,
Breathe living air in me —
To them my doors are open wide and free.

I open my eyes on passing mountain scenes,*
Then close my lids
And race in mental aerial plane
To view again the unseen world of souls:
Cities loom, with passions all;
Liquid mazes of desires,
Deceiving mires;
Ego's dark, titanic chasms,
Where faith has never shone.

What lands pass I?
Whose kingdom see?
There, in the land of minds,
And there alone, I find
The real America, the living India;
The beauties and the barren tracts
Of nations all, of souls all.
Yet diverse though this kingdom be,
There lives here but One Reality.

Three thousand miles of land I traveled not,

* Paramahansaji wrote these verses while riding in a car
through the countryside near Denver, Colorado.

But through three thousand miles of minds
　　was brought.
I find writ
And well knit
In outer scenes —
Fields, gardens, cities, shops —
The thought vibrations of those myriad minds.
How oft men pass, unheeding, all the beauties
Of familiar paths, and sheltering trees;
In blindness they roam
In the garden of hearts.
In them I long to start
A vision new:
Of Beauty, eternal and true.

VARIETY

I sought for twins,
But could not find.
I search my mind;
No twins I've seen.

They seem alike —
Man and man, beast and brute —
Yet no faces two are like;
Ne'er the same song sang the lute.

Thy debut, O Eternity,
Was limitless in its diversity —
To that Deity of the New in things
My spirit homage sings.

Since ne'er two hearts are same,
I bow to each new form and name.
Variety complete,
Through patterns infinite.

I wish that I were you and he,
And all at once this changing me
Would be whate'er I'd be,
Like donning robes of newer kinds —
If I could wear at will all terrene minds.

Then would I flash forth varied smiles,

Or languorous walk in sorrow robed,
Or charm with sparkling wiles
To time beguile;
Or march with martial songs,
To right all worldly wrongs;
Or wield a powerful prophet mind
And into dust earth's sorrows grind.
Or with a youthful hermit's heart
I'd scatter love and strength impart.

I'd wear each heart
And don each will and smile, and spend my pelf
To try all noble minds and thoughts,
And take what suits myself.

With brain-born nixes,
With will-o'-the-wisp hopes
And mental-marsh marauding pixies,
With every elfin thought
That timid treads on mind
I'd friendship find.

My spirit clings
To the new in things—
I would not taste the same nectar,
Though twice I drink from the immortals' jar.

Thy presence, O Eternity,
Show Thou in endless variety;

Yet change not me —
Though various my costumes be.

Keep me the humble same,
Whatever be my name;
And let me watch myself
In changeless mirror of my Self.

Thou and I, our dress will change
Yet Thou and I will never change.

ON COMING TO THE NEW-OLD
LAND—AMERICA

Sleeping memories,
Of friends once more to be,
Did greet me — sailing o'er the sea —
Sensing my coming,
The Pilgrim Land to adore.

The distant sleeping shore
Lay in the twinkling night,
Dim through the vanished light.
The breeze wafted strong;
    Strange thoughts
    My brain did throng,
    Hopes sweet and richly wrought.

A raven-wingèd gloom did perch
On portals of my mind, to search
My soul, my strength to awe;
    But then with joy what crowds I saw,
    Of phantom friends
    Now come to lend
    Their cheer,
    And end my fear!

YOGODA DREAM HERMITAGE — A
DREAM DROPPED FROM HEAVEN

A vision of yore — of incarnations before —
Of a dream-bud retreat
Grew in the garden of my soul.
For ages 'twas caressed,
By sun-warm breeze of His blessings blessed,
Until in this life,
Away from all strife,
Beyond noises' reach,
On Encinitas' mountain-beach
That dream-bud blossomed true.
A dream of silent rest
Dropped down from Heaven's breast,
Through magic touch of one, most blessed of mine!
Beloved Saint Lynn* divine.

The muted mystery fragrance of this flower-home
Long midst evolving cosmic dreams did roam.
At last it came wafting — enchanting, entrancing —
Down the arches of the ancient years;
And then a glimpse, through vaporous joyous tears,
Leading me to search the golden California coast, here
   and there —

---

* Mr. James J. Lynn. An exalted disciple of Paramahansaji,
he later received from his guru the monastic title and name,
Rajarsi Janakananda.

North, east, west, south — everywhere.
Divine Mother's whispered call
Then summoned me to sea-cliff bold — a motionless
   mountain-liner tall —
With decks of rocks and caves, and many a lacy tree —
Jutting out to sea,
Anchored forever
By sands of silver.

Seated on sandy mound,
Surf-tapestried opal ocean 'round —
Ecstatic, heaven-bound —
Like a diamond-flash, this retreat I found
Glistening on the screen
Of my forehead's Spirit-Eye unseen.

Divine Mother asked me to look and see
If I could find Her close by the hills of Elsinore.*
But now I shall seek Her no more
In any other sea-fenced mountain core;
For Dame Divinity I found reigning
Within, without, everywhere — bliss-showers
    raining—
By enrapturing Encinitas' elysian shore.

---

* Prompted by the inner vision that he would someday have an ashram near the sea, Paramahansaji had in earlier years searched near Lake Elsinore for the right place to build a hermitage. However, the Encinitas bluff overlooking the sea had remained his favorite place of meditation, and it was for this reason that Rajarsi chose this spot for construction of Paramahansaji's "dream hermitage."

INVISIBLE MOTHER

O Thou Mother of all,
Be Thou consciously receptive to my prayers.
All that I know, I know through Thee;
And Thou knowest all I know,
So Thou knowest my prayers.
Knowing Thee, feeling Thee constantly,
I know Thou art I, I am Thou.
The little wavelet of me has vanished in Thee.

Thou alone didst exist
Before Thy maya waves appeared;
And Thou alone dost exist now, and ever shall —
Naught is, that is not Thee.
Formless, impersonal Thou art;
The Unseen, omnipresent.
But I want to know Thee also, and forever,
As personal.

In the gaze of my devotion I behold Thee:
Sometimes as Krishna,
Sometimes as Christ,
Personal, visible — imprisoned
In the little form
Hidden within the temple of my love.

O Mother Invisible, as Thou didst freeze
Thine unseen Infinitude

Into the sea of cosmic finitude,
Do Thou appear to me
In visible, living form,
That I may adore and serve Thee.
I want to see Thee, the Ocean of Life,
With and without Thy ripples of finite creation.
O Creator of all things, I want to worship Thee
As both personal and impersonal.

ONE FRIEND

Many clouds do race to hide Thee —
Of friends and wealth and fame —
And yet through mist of tears I see
Appear Thy Golden Name.
Each time my father, mother, friends
Do loudly claim they did me tend,
I wake from sleep to sweetly hear
That Thou alone didst help me here.

TWO BLACK EYES

When my brother or my teacher
Stormed at me,
In the haven of my mother's two black eyes
I found my retreat.
She died —
And I cried —
And I sought those lost two eyes everywhere.
I searched in the stars,
Until, bedimmed by my tears,
They twinkled black eyes everywhere.
But they were not those that I lost!
There were many black eyes
That sought to mother me,
But they were not those that I loved!
Looking, searching for her everywhere,
I found my Divine Mother;
And in Her love
I found my mother's love;
And in Her omnipresent eyes,
I found those lost two black eyes.

MY COSMIC MOTHER'S FACE

Fairy dream faces, like fresh flowers,
May bloom in the vase of my gaze for my soul
    to see;
But the Face that vanished behind space
Cannot be replaced by any of these.

There are faces of transcendent beauty,
Faces of exquisite charm, faces tender and true;
There are faces of sweetness and wisdom,
But there's none like the face of You.

There are faces tainted by fires of lust,
Faces the wise cannot fathom, faces a child
    cannot trust.
There are faces of beauty, steeped in glory
    through and through;
But, O Cosmic Mother, they are dim beside You.

There's the violet, the lily, the lotus, the rose;
Fragrant flower-faces blooming under the snows;
There are faces of stars, and the moon
    and the sun,
But for me there's One Face evermore, only one.

After my search through aeons unnumbered,
The never-ceasing streamlets of my dreams
Have melted in Thy silver ocean-face,

Where smiling love forever softly gleams.

Countless silver rays of living beauties
Have melted into one transcendent grace —
The beauties of a million, million ages —
To make, at last, Thine omnipresent face.

Without Thy face, there is no light for me
In all the unplumbed depths of land or sea;
Thy beauty-rays are rainbowed over all
Eternity, while planets rise and fall.

On the lips of laughter, on roses in the dawn,
It is Thy smile forever glowing there —
An immortelle of glory, heavenly sweet
With fragrance of unceasing, selfless prayer.

On the calm lake of my breathless bosom,
Where ripplets of desire no more
Play little games like children,
The glimmer of Thy face is spreading o'er.

In the cleansed mirror of my memory,
In the deep crystal pool that is my heart,
I see Thine omnipresence trapped for me —
Of my own self forevermore a part.

As I, awakening, pass through gates of light,
Thy wisdom-face is all my soul can see.

Faded, the pale pleasure-stars of dream skies,
In the omniscient light enfolding Thee.*

Auroras, lights squeezed from shimmering hives
    of atoms,
Flashing feelings, burning vitalities, worlds
    of flame,
Dumb stones and speaking minds — all
    melted together
To form Thy one face and to spell Thy one name.

My vision, withdrawn from viewing pulsating
    centuries,
Throws its countless eyes within to search
    eternity;
And all I seek, O Cosmic Mother, all I crave
    forever,
Is the light of one face — the face of Thee!

* As the divine consciousness in man awakens, it disconnects itself from the senses and moves upward through the "gates of light" (the *chakras,* or centers of light and superconsciousness in the spine) to the altar of Spirit in the "thousand-petaled lotus" in the brain, where one beholds the "omniscient light" of God.

BREATHE IN ME

Breathe in me the way to love You,
That I may learn to faultlessly love You.
Pour me the wisdom-wine
By which I become intoxicated with You.
Whisper in my ears of silence
The way to be with You always.
Speak to my wandering senses
And lead them back to Your sanctuary within.
Call the marauding mind and counsel it
How to retrace its steps to Your home.
With Your silent eyes, just look at me,
And I will know where to find You.

You may hide behind the ocean,
You may hide behind delusion,
You may hide behind life,
You may hide behind dualities,
You may hide behind theological conundrums,
You may hide behind unanswered prayers,
But You cannot hide behind my love,
For in the mirroring light of my love
You are revealed.

THE SPLINTERS OF THY LOVE

The splinters of Thy love
Lie strewn in many a heart.
These little fragments of Thy love,
Descended from far above,
I find spread here and there; and charmed, I start
To seize all and with care collect.
I feel, as I reflect,
That I have certes seen somewhere
Thy whole unbroken love that's everywhere;
And with devotion strong
I weld my varied collection
Of tiny bits of friendly and parental love in one,
To match it with Thine own.

WHAT IS LOVE?

Love is the scent with the lotus born.
It is the silent choirs of petals
Singing the winter's harmony of uniform beauty.
Love is the song of the soul, singing to God.
It is the balanced rhythmic dance of planets—
    sun and moon lit
In the skyey hall festooned with fleecy clouds—
Around the sovereign Silent Will.
It is the thirst of the rose to drink the sunrays
And blush red with life.
'Tis the promptings of the mother earth
To feed her milk to the tender, thirsty roots,
And to nurse all life.
It is the urge of the sun
To keep all things alive.

Love is the unseen craving of the Mother Divine
That took the protecting father-form,
And that feeds helpless mouths
With milk of mother's tenderness.
It is the babies' sweetness,
Coaxing the rain of parental sympathy
To shower upon them.
It is the lover's unenslaved surrender to the beloved
To serve and solace.
It is the elixir of friendship,
Reviving broken and bruised souls.

It is the martyr's zeal to shed his blood
For the well-beloved fatherland.
It is the ineffable, silent call of the heart to another
    heart.
It is the God-drunk poet's heartaches
For every creature's groans.

Love is to enjoy the family rose of petal-beings,
And thence to move to spacious fields —
Passing by portals of social, national, international
    sympathy,
On to the limitless Cosmic Home —
To gaze with looks of wonderment,
And to serve all that lives, still or moving.
This is to know what love is.
He knows who lives it.

Love is evolution's ameliorative call
To the far-strayed sons
To return to Perfection's home.
It is the call of the beauty-robed ones
To worship the great Beauty.
It is the call of God
Through silent intelligences
And starbursts of feelings.

Love is the Heaven
Toward which the flowers, rivers, nations, atoms,
    creatures — you and I

Are rushing by the straight path of action right,
Or winding laboriously on error's path,
All to reach haven there at last.

A MILK-WHITE SAIL

A milk-white, tiny sail
Skims fast across my sea; I wail,
The threatening storm to see.
But swift my bark glides free, toward the lee;
So near the Shore,
'Tis safe from tempest's angry roar.

THE LITTLE ETERNITY

As a dream melts deep
Into the silent well of sleep,
So may this earthly dreaming
Dissolve in the depth of Thy being.
To fly from dream to dream,
Nightmare to nightmare;
And from birth to rebirth,
Death to repeated deaths,
Seems useless, hazardous traveling
When, behind the wings of Thy blessings,
My soul can be safe in Thy keeping.

The universe, so big through the eyes,
Is only a tiny slimy egg of thought
Beaten with the egg-beater of fancy,
Frothed up into this fluffy cosmic dream—
With sextillion worlds glimmering,
With Milky Way bubbles shimmering.
The giant cosmic lot
Throbs and lives in a single little thought.
The vast cosmic dream—albeit
Squeezed into tiniest nothingness—
Can be eternally expanded, tier upon tier,
Into an ever-growing, endless sphere.

My body with the universe-name,
And my little, finite frame,

Both recede or reside
In my thought's ebb and tide.
The colossal cosmic God
Somehow lives on my little self's sod;
And I, a tiny being,
Am in His palace of eternity living.
He lives in me; Him as my home I use.
He dreams in me; and in Him I muse.
He is awake in me, and I was asleep in Him.
He dies in me when I sleep in delusion;
He is reborn in my wisdom-womb's seclusion.
Sleeps the little eternity
In my measureless amity.

THE TATTERED DRESS

I see Thy magic hands of death
Snatch away in stealth
And change the tattered dress—
Which fondly men caress
With blind attachment—
Into soul-sheen habiliment:
A newly given robe,
That shines with th' empyrean beauties
Of Thy globe.

LUTHER BURBANK

Beatific Burbank!
The great reformer Luther, thou art,
Of living plants and flowers of every mood—
The tender ones, the stubborn-growing ones,
Or cactus rude.

Thy peaceful ways
The cruel cactus took:
Its armor of thorns forsook,

And learned to sacrifice its meat
For all to eat.

Eight-score years it took the hard-shelled
    stubborn walnut tree to fully grow;
Thy care did soften its shell and taught it
    seven-score years to throw.

The flowerlike smile upon thy face
Tells thou wert nurtured at Nature's breast,
Bedecked with petals' lace.

I saw thee
As a God-grown mental lotus-flower,
Opening tenderly
To cast the beauty rays
Of thy plant knowledge — its supreme ways —
On thy fellow man;
And also turning gently to the mighty Invisible Sun
That lights little plants, distant stars, the
    bursting bubble, thee and me and man.

Thou didst not ask, "Who art thou?"
But understood my speaking heart.
Our souls touched, and we saw
We had one goal, one task, one law:
By knowledge to break
The walls of dogma dark.

On the Ocean's surface is diversity;
Beneath lie all the waves in Unity.
We both dived deep:
Thou, through living waves of plants,
And I through waves of human minds.
We found we met beneath,
As all deep divers may,
In the vast expanse of Unity;
In the great Truth-sea.

Thou dost dread isms and dogmas
And I all man-made false enigmas.
We "outcasts" know but one bright
Truth-made path of light.
  Men go not in;
  That's why they say,
  "He's far away, oh, far away."
  He dost not hide from us,
  But we from Him.
  Let's rush,
  Within let's go —
  Lo! He's there alway.

God didst make thee, and all, in His image.
Certes thou hast broken the dogma of ages:
By creating new fruits, new plants,
Thou showest the world in wonder
The Creator's child a creator.

O Santa Rosa, thou art blessed
To have blown the perfume of this great flower
That all people of the earth enjoy its shower
Of scent so sweet.

If Nature makes some imperfect plant,
Burbank by his magic wand
Its invading germs disbands.
He creates new kinds from old—
With new coats, quickened in color and growth.
There's a suggestion for you, dear world,
That his life imparts:
If weak, afflicted, or error-fixed thou art,
Thou canst— if thy reason starts
In the direction right,
With determined might
To become all free—
Be what thy soul wishes and works to be.

Santa Rosa, thy Luther-flower the ages shall
    not fade;
In soil of memories shall it live, e'er fresh,
Through endless decades.

FRIENDSHIP

Is friendship the weaving of the red strings
  of two hearts?
Is it the blending of two minds into a spacious
  one mind?
Is it the spouting of love founts together
To strengthen the rush of love on droughty souls?
Is it the one rose grown 'twixt twin mind-branchlets
Of one compassionate stem?
Is it the one thinking in two bodies?

Or is friendship like two strong stallions,
Disparate in color and mien,
Pulling the chariot of life together
To the one Goal, with one mind-sight?

Is friendship founded on equalities or inequalities?
Is it built on diverse stones of differences?
Is friendship unthinking agreement—
The hand-in-hand blind walking of two souls,
Foolishly rejoicing in their united folly,
Falling at last into pits of disillusionment?

Friendship is noble, fruitful, holy—
When two separate souls march in difference
Yet in harmony; agreeing and disagreeing,
Glowingly improving diversely,

With a common longing to find solace in true
   pleasure.

When ne'er the lover seeks
Self-comfort at cost of the one beloved,
Then, in that garden of selflessness,
Fragrant friendship perfectly flowers.
For friendship is a hybrid, born of two souls —
The blended fragrance of two unlike flowers
Blown together in love's caressing breeze.

Friendship is born from the very core
Of secret inexplicable likings.
Friendship is the fountain of true feelings.
It grows in both likeness and difference.
Friendship sleeps or dies in familiarity,
And decays in lusts of narrow-eyed selves.
Friendship grows tall and sturdy
In the soil of oneness in body, mind, and soul.

Demands, deceptions, sordid sense of possession,
Courtesy's lack, narrow self-love, suspicion,
Thoughtless, sharp-pointed, piercing words —
Cankers, these, which eat at the heart of friendship.

Ah, friendship — flowering, heaven-born plant!
Nurtured art thou in the soil of measureless love,
In the seeking of soul progress together

By two who would smooth the way, each for
   the other.
Watered art thou by attentions of affection
And the tender dews of inner and outer sweetness
Of the selfless heart's inmost devotion.

Ah, friendship! where thy soul-born flowers fall,
There, on that sacred shrine of fragrance,
The Friend of all friends craves to come,
   and to remain.

MY KINSMEN

In spacious hall of trance,
Aglow with million dazzling lights,
Tapestried with snowy cloud,
I spied my kinsmen all — the lowly, proud.

The banquet great with music swelled,
The drum of Aum* in measure fell.
The guests in many ways arrayed,
Some plain, some gorgeous dress displayed.

Around the various tables large
Of earth and moon and sun and stars,
The countless mute or noisy guests
Observed Dame Nature's feast with zest.

The tiny-eyed and shiny sands,
Thirsty, drank of ocean's life:
I well remember once I brawled
For a sip of sea, with kinsmen sands.

Yes, I know those old dame rocks
Who held me on their stony laps
When I, a tiny baby tree,
Did chafe to run with winds so free.

* Cosmic creative vibration.

87

The green-attirèd friends I know,
With rose and lily buds aglow;
I once adorned a kingly breast—
Lost life; returned to mother dust.

I know the ruby's red breast dear,
My blood in it once flowed so clear;
I smiled in diamonds, gleaming bright,
I danced in roentgen rays of light.

A ray of friendship from my heart,
In diamond and ruby joy did start;
The bright one smiled, the ruby wept,
To meet their long-lost friend at last.

The soul of gold in yellow gown,
The soul of silver in white robe shone,
Bestowed on me maternal smiles
That told they knew me long erewhile.

The leafy fingers, arms outspread,
Caressed me when a tiny bird,
And fed me with ambrosial fruit
That drew its life from immortal root.

The lark, the cuckoo, the pheasant sweet,
The deer, the lamb, the lion great,
The shark and monsters of the sea,
In love and peace all greeted me.

When first the atoms and stardust sprang,
When Vedas, Bible, Koran sang,
I joined each choir; their long-past thrilling songs
Still echo in my soul in accents strong.

I AM HE

Based on Swami Shankara's chant

No birth, no death, no caste have I;
Father, mother, have I none:
I am He, I am He — blessed Spirit, I am He!
Mind, nor intellect, nor ego, feeling;
Sky, nor earth, nor metals am I:
I am He, I am He — blessed Spirit, I am He!
Not *prana,* or its vital currents five,
Nor the quintuple sheaths of wisdom traits and
    body-stuff,*
Nor flesh, or senses that enthrall,
Nor ether, fire, or air withal — am I.
I am He, I am He, soul of wisdom, I am He!
Bondage I do not fear; for freedom I do not care,
For I am free, ever free; I am free, ever free:
I am He, I am He — blessed Spirit, I am He!

* *Prana* is the intelligent life energy that pervades and sustains
the human body through the specialized functions of five
currents. The "quintuple sheaths" are the five *koshas* or subtle
coverings that separate the soul in delusion from Spirit.

TO THE AURORA BOREALIS

Over Forest Lake, Minneapolis, Minnesota

From the heart of the northern horizon,
A dim, palpitating fountain of flame
Spread flickeringly
Through the dark stray clouds and the Milky Way,
And across the space o'erhead.
Softly glowing, liquid fleecy lights
Rose, quivered, and flooded the southern land.
Aurora lit the sky,
And played with shadows within the deeps
   of the limpid lake —
Fluttered scintillating, transparent lights
O'er the stars and the sky o'erhead;
And shone on the rippleless lake beneath —
Then floated like dream waves of light
In my mental sea.*

Stilled thoughts, like stars, would glimmer
Through dim mental clouds;
Wisdom's aurora-light would rise from medulla's
   horizon

---

* While observing the phenomenon of the aurora, Paramahansaji experienced a corresponding inner vision. In this
poetic rendering, he makes a comparison between his exter-
nal perception of the beauty of the aurora and the glory and
expansion of his internal state of *samadhi*, or God-
consciousness.

And spread, tremblingly, lighting
The dark vapors of mind.
Thou matchless lone imitator of all these —
O Aurora!
Spreader of light and joy o'er cloudy hearts,
Reminder, thou, of bursting, glowing light
 within my forehead!

From the left and right extreme, invisible lamps
Threw sudden iridescent red or blue sky-kissing
 searchlights,
Spouting ethereal mystic flames,
Which joyfully bounded and vanished in the
 Eternal Ray.
Ever-burning radium, thou, Aurora!

My inner fountain of strange colors
Flooded my mental sky,
Illumining the opaque darkness
Behind which the Light of all lights hides.
A vision it was, of ever-changing, rolling,
 molten light,
Coaxing the stars, trees, water, earth, and
 matter, all
To melt their grossness
And become the Cosmic Light.

Aurora, there is hope,
For I shall liquefy in my *samadhi's* fire

All grossness of my mortal being,
And all creation's dust.
Matter shall change to light;
Darkness will burst into atoms of leaping fire.
My little soul will breathe with the Eternal
 Breath—
With the birth of each breath, new solar
 systems will be born;
And as each breath of eternity escapes from me,
Many a universe will cease to breathe.
The feeling bounded by the body will fly free
To feel the universe.
No more shall I clasp but a little clod;
In my bosom I shall bear the burden
Of the twinkling atomic vapors of nebulae,
Shining stars, planets, and all living things.
For I am the Life,
And my body is the universe.
Smaller am I than all little things made—
I can hide behind a speck of electron—
And bigger am I than the sphere in which the
 cosmos breathes.
I am the Life that shattered its confines of littleness
To become the infinite bigness of all things.

I am the most subtle — the subtlest of forces
 is gross enough to hide me—
Yet everything speaks of me.
I wake with the dawn,

I exercise my vital muscular rays in the sun;
I sleep in the night,
Or oft peep through the twinkling lights in the
    darkness.
I smile in the moon,
I heave in the ocean.
I paint and wipe away
The pictures on the canvas of the sky.
I make the dewdrop, and conjure the flowers
    with my invisible wand.
I whistle in the canaries and sing in the
    nightingales.
I melt and sigh in human breasts.
I whisper through conscience.
I roar in the thunder.
I work in the noisy wheels of factories.
And I play hide and seek with the sky, stars,
    clouds, and waters,
As the mystic light of the aurora.

SAMADHI*

Vanished are the veils of light and shade,
Lifted the vapors of sorrow,
Sailed away the dawn of fleeting joy,
Gone the mirage of the senses.
Love, hate, health, disease, life and death —
Departed, these false shadows on the screen
   of duality.
Waves of laughter, scyllas of sarcasm, whirlpools
   of melancholy,
Melting in the vast sea of bliss.
Bestilled is the storm of maya

* *Samadhi*, literally, "to direct together," is the state of
oneness of human consciousness with Cosmic Consciousness
in meditation. Being subject to relativity, human consciousness experiences the duality of separateness from God. Thus
we have the consciousness of the meditator, the act of meditation, and God (as the object of meditation). The end result of
deep, continuous, rightly performed meditation is *samadhi*,
the blissful state in which these three factors become one.
Just as the wave becomes one with the sea, so the human soul
experiences its identity with Spirit.

During the lifetime of Paramahansa Yogananda, this poem
was in circulation in more than one version. All were quite
similar, reflecting only minor variations introduced by Paramahansaji. The most familiar rendering has been in print for
many years in his *Autobiography of a Yogi*. Publication of this
volume of *Songs of the Soul* has provided an appropriate
vehicle in which to keep in print another representative
rendering. (*Publisher's Note*)

By the magic wand of intuition deep.
The universe, a forgotten dream, lurks
    subconsciously,
Ready to invade my newly wakened memory divine.
I exist without the cosmic shadow,
But it could not live bereft of me;
As the sea exists without the waves,
But they breathe not without the sea.
Dreams, wakings, states of deep *turiya** sleep,
Present, past, future, no more for me,
But the ever-present, all-flowing I, I, everywhere.
Consciously enjoyable,
Beyond the imagination of all expectancy,
Is this, my *samadhi* state.
Planets, stars, stardust, earth,
Volcanic bursts of doomsday cataclysms,
Creation's molding furnace,
Glaciers of silent X-rays,
Burning floods of electrons,
Thoughts of all men, past, present, future,
Every blade of grass, myself and all,
Each particle of creation's dust,
Anger, greed, good, bad, salvation, lust,

---

* Superconsciousness; the fourth state, beyond waking, dreaming, and deep sleep. Here *turiya* is used poetically to refer to the glimpse of superconscious peace in the state of deep dreamless sleep.

I swallowed up — transmuted them
Into one vast ocean of blood of my own one Being!
Smoldering joy, oft-puffed by unceasing meditation,
Which blinded my tearful eyes,
Burst into eternal flames of bliss,
And consumed my tears, my peace, my frame,
　　my all.
Thou art I, I am Thou,
Knowing, Knower, Known, as One!
One tranquilled, unbroken thrill of eternal, living,
　　ever-new peace!

Not an unconscious state
Or mental chloroform without wilful return,
Samadhi but extends my realm of consciousness
Beyond the limits of my mortal frame
To the boundaries of eternity,
Where I, the Cosmic Sea,
Watch the little ego floating in Me.
Not a sparrow, nor a grain of sand, falls
　　without my sight.
All space floats like an iceberg in my mental sea.
I am the Colossal Container of all things made!
By deeper, longer, continuous, thirsty,
　　guru-given meditation,
This celestial *samadhi* is attained.
All the mobile murmurs of atoms are heard;
The dark earth, mountains, seas are molten liquid!
This flowing sea changes into vapors of nebulae!

Aum blows o'er the vapors; they open their veils,
Revealing a sea of shining electrons,
Till, at the last sound of the cosmic drum,
Grosser light vanishes into eternal rays
Of all-pervading Cosmic Joy.
From Joy we come,
For Joy we live,
In the sacred Joy we melt.
I, the ocean of mind, drink all creation's waves.
The four veils of solid, liquid, vapor, light,
Lift aright.
Myself, in everything,
Enters the Great Myself.
Gone forever,
The fitful, flickering shadows of a mortal memory.
Spotless is my mental sky,
Below, ahead, and high above.
Eternity and I, one united ray.
I, a tiny bubble of laughter,
Have become the Sea of Mirth Itself.

IN ME

Hello, yonder tree!
Thou dost breathe in me, in me.
O fast-footed river!
Thy shining, meandering quiver
Declares itself
Through myself;
Thou dost shine through me, in me.

O huge Himalaya
With snowy sovereign white regalia!
In my mind doth rest thy throne —
Thy home in me, in me.

O ocean endless to the eye!
In boundless stretches thou dost lie;
But thou to me art small —
A tiny drop upon a ball —
Thou art in me, in me.

O infinite sky!
So vast to mortal eye,
In some brighter age or day
When I'll cast my cares away,
My better boat — free, shining, gay —
On thee will sail
Unto thy shore
To find, I'm sure,

Thy borderland — in me.

O distant heavens!
O secret One and angels seven!
In my sphere You all I see,
In me, in me, in me!

TOO NEAR

I stood in silence to worship Thee
In Thy temple grand —
With blue etheric dome,
Lighted by the spangling stars,
Shining with the lustrous moon,
Tapestried with golden clouds —
Where reigns no dogma loud.
I prayed and waited
For Thee to come. I cried —
Thou didst not come.
I'll wait no more,
Nor send my feeble prayer,
Footsteps Thine to hear.

They are not heard without:
In me Thou art — too near.

DIVINE LOVE SORROWS

The music of Fritz Kreisler's "Liebesleid" inspired Paramahansaji to write these words for it.

I have been roaming, forsaken by Thee,
Who hast seen me groping,
Hardly ever answering.
I shall be roaming, roaming,
Bursting all boundaries of heart,
Evermore moving toward Thee,
To Thy vast unthrobbing heart.

Come Thou to me, O Lord!
Oh, come at last to me!
Centuries and centuries
I have waited now for Thee.
Through endless incarnations
I called out for Thy name,
Searching by the streamlets
Of all my silvery dreams.

I knew that Thou must come at last
To steal the flowers of my heart.
In sorrow thrills I piped my love,
I sadly sang my song to Thee.
And yet I knew my love would reach Thee,
Though many lives I had to wait.
On mountain crags of high devotion
I sadly sang my song, my song, my song.

MY MOTHER'S EYES

Whence came the black-eyed light,
Flickering in my life a moment?
Whither did it flit away?
The twilight of many incarnations
Had glowed in those eyes;
Many lights of love dreams
Had met in the bower of those two eyes.
And then, only the soulless altar—
The lifeless eyes—
Remained before me.

Thou Secret Queen,
From what unknown region

Didst Thou in silence come
To bewitch the fortress of those eyes?
Many a time,
By bitter speech and sadness driven,
The boat of my life found safety
In the harbor of those two eyes.

And now the cruel death-quake has forever marred
Those dream-harboring eyes.
Losing the harbor of those eyes,
In search I sailed my boat
In the sea of the sky.
Threefold sorrow storm-driven,
This life-boat of mine
Had become motherless!
My boat sailed on directionless,
In the uncharted regions of the vast sky-sea
Seeking those two lost eyes
Among the star-eyed lights.
All starry eyes
Twinkled black eyes
But they were not those
I had lost.

Merely affection-saturated,
Many black eyes called to me,
Offering to nurse my motherless sorrow —
This orphan life of mine.
But none matched the love-call glance

Of the lost two dark eyes.
The love of those two black eyes
Forever had set
From the region of all black eyes
That I beheld.

Seeking the lost two eyes
In birth and death,
In life and dreams,
And in all the lands of the unknown,
At last I found
The all-pervading Divine Mother's
Countless black eyes—
In space and heart,
In earth-cores, in stars,
Within and without,
Hungrily staring at me
From everywhere.

Seeking and seeking my dead mother,
I found the Deathless Mother.
The lost love of my earthly mother
I found in my Cosmic Mother.
Seeking and searching,
In Her countless black eyes
I found those lost two black eyes.
I asked my Mother Divine:
"With ruthless heart,
Why didst Thou tear away

The dazzling diamond of my mother's love
From the ring of my heart?"

The cloud voice of Mother Divine
Burst through the firmament within:
"Many times have I fed thee
The life-blood of My milk
From the breasts of many mothers.
Your black-eyed mother,
Whom you lost awhile,
Was none else but Me, only Me.
When I saw that thy wisdom and cosmic love
Had lost their way
In the dark jungle of those two eyes,
I set afire that alluring darkness.*
I stole away those imprisoning two black eyes
That thou might'st be free
To find those eyes
In My eyes,
And in the eyes of all black-eyed mothers;
And that thou might'st behold,
In all black eyes,
Shadows only of My eyes.
I broke the finite, dream-made
'Thy mother' form of Mine
That thou might'st behold Me,
Thy Divine Mother,
In the form of every soulful woman
And in My Infinite Cosmic Form."

* Reference to the custom in India of cremation of the dead.

THOU IN ME

When I smile,
Thou dost smile through me;
When I cry,
In me Thou dost weep.

When I wake,
Thou greetest me;
When I walk,
Thou art with me.

Thou dost smile and weep,
Thou dost wake and walk, like me—
My likeness, Thou.

But when I dream,
Thou art awake;
When I stumble,
Thou art sure;
When I die,
Thou art my life.

THE GREAT LIGHTLAND

I have been roaming in Endlessness
In the fire-mist of the great Lightland.
In that Luminosity
I read the meaning of all mysteries
Scribbled on the scrolls of time.
I am half-awakenedly
Enjoying the dream of earth-life;
And while I am dreaming
I sip the joys
From the cup of delicious meditations.
O Blessedness,
Walk with me in my kingdom
Of royal happiness,
And keep me from the dream-nightmare
    of trialsome life.

THY HOMECOMING

This vision I had during an ecstatic state of God-realization. I saw myself sitting on a little patch of the Milky Way, beholding the vast universe around me. As God became manifest, all things that had before seemed inanimate were consciously celebrating His homecoming within my consciousness — in the mansion of light.

God has been banished from your consciousness by ignorance. That is why you think you are circumscribed by a little mortal body; that is why you cannot behold the universe as it really is, ablaze with the life and joy of Spirit. When I celebrated God's homecoming within my own consciousness, I saw that the whole cosmos was a part of that realization.

Thy mansion of the heavens is lit by perennial
    auroral displays of mystic lights.
Stellar systems arch across the trackless highways of
    eternity that lead to Thy secret home.
Comet-peacocks spread their plumes of rays and
    dance in wild delight in Thy garden of many
    moons.
The planetary dance glides in stately rhythm,
    awaiting Thy homecoming.
I sit on a little patch of the Milky Way and behold
    the glory of Thy kingdom spread round me —
    endlessly, everywhere.
The festivities of the heavens are dazzling with
    fireworks of shooting stars — hurled across the
    blue vaults by unseen bands of Thine obedient,
    devoted forces.

Meteorites skip, glow, swoon, and fall to earth —
mad with Thy joy.

Everybody, everything, every atom, rejoices in
proclaiming Thee the uncrowned King of the
Universes.

Each day the trees drop flowers in Thine honor, and
the skyey vase sends wisps of fire-mist incense to
Thee.

Candlesticks of heavenly powers hold incandescent
stars to light Thy temple.

Because Thou didst hide Thyself away — banished
by Thy subjects' ignorance — Thy mansion of
matter has been dark.

Now darkness is being dispelled, and all the
gloom-drenched chambers in Thy domain of
eternity are becoming radiant at the news of Thy
return.

Heavenly lights have opened their gates. Bonfires of
nebulous mists are heralding Thine approach.

The steady sentinels of sun and moon are patiently
waiting for Thy homecoming.

And I — I am running wild, dancing in my little
body on my little earth, or skimming over the
Milky Way, coaxing everything, every atom,
every speck of consciousness, to open its gates
and let Thy light shine through completely,
driving darkness forevermore from Thy cosmic
kingdom, which without Thee was a lonesome
wilderness of matter.

THE CUP OF ETERNITY

The traveler of the endless track,
All weary, thirsty, sore doth seek
To quench the quenchless mortal thirst,
The wordless worry of his heart.

He spies a cup — a little orb —
And hies to drink with joyful sob.
Then stands aback, the cup sets down;
On contents scant his heart doth frown.

Yet up he lifts the cup again,
But fears his baneful thirst to flame.
When, hark! a voice of counsel deep
Forbids him this to soil with lip.

The cup so small to mundane eye,
(Whose depth the wise alone can spy)
Dries up, alas, if mortals drink;
(Perennial fount, the soulful think.)

Now, in the little cup he'll see
Th' unsounded deep of eternity;
For ageless hours and endless days
The ambrosial drink he'll taste and praise.

The deathly thirst so fleshly born
Shall parch his soul, oh, ne'er again!

The cup he'll drink, but not the bane,
To quench his thirst and bliss attain.*

And vain would mighty north winds try
Compassion's gathered tears to dry.
For other thirsting souls he'll weep,
And beg them, "From the cup, drink deep!"

---

* At first the cup of true bliss seems to possess "contents scant" (the quietude of meditation seems a barren substitute for material interests). But by the exercise of true discrimination and right choice of pleasures, man begins to experience the illimitable nature of divine joy and to discover the infinite treasures within the "little orb" of his spiritual eye (the "single eye" referred to by Christ), the true "cup of eternity."

AT THE FOUNTAIN OF SONG

Dig, dig, yet deeper dig
The stony earth for fount of song;
Dig, dig, yet deeper dig,
The soil of muse's heart along.

Some sparkle is seen,
Some bubble is heard;
'Tis then unseen—
The bubble is dead.

The watery sheen
Again doth show;
Dig, dig, still deeper e'en,
Till the bubble-song again doth grow.

I hear the song,
I see its bubble-body bright;
Yet cannot touch. Oh, how I long
To seize it now,
And drink its liquid light!
Bleed, O my soul, do amply bleed
To dig yet deeper — dig!

To fountain's mystic song
My soul is drawn;
In violin tones it plays
In endless lays.
Oft I thought, What strains are left to sing?
Yet newer songs it dared to bring.

I touch the holy fount, rejoice —
I drink its bubble voice.
My throat's ablaze;
I want to drink and drink always.

The sphere's aflame —
With flaming thirst I came;
"Dig, dig, yet deeper dig,"
   I said,
"Though it seems Thou canst not dig."

I thought, with heart aglow,
All, all, I'd drunk this day;
But still, I idly looked for more — deep,
   deep, below.
And lo! undrunk, untouched,
There the fountain lay.*

* This poem hints at the indescribable experiences of a yogi
as he follows the inner fountain of song: the melodic variations of the sound of the Cosmic Aum — the Word, or great
Amen — manifesting in the *chakras*, or spiritual centers of
consciousness, within man's spine. The "stony earth," the
"watery sheen," and the "sphere aflame" refer respectively to
the earth, water, and fire *chakras*. Once the yogi has tran-
scended these three lower centers, his inward "digging," or
deeper meditation, quickly carries him upward through the
remaining three *chakras* — of air, ether, and etheric bliss — to
cosmic consciousness.

The opening of each *chakra* reveals ever-new and
undreamed-of beauties; overwhelming bliss descends on the
persevering devotee. Entering the infinite kingdom of God,
he is enthralled by its inexhaustible glories.

PIKES PEAK

Ne'er did I expect to roam
On wheels four
Where thousand clouds do soar—
The dangerous, darksome path
With tricky winding "W" curves that climbed
And glided secretly
Full fourteen thousand feet above the sea—
The home of dark-hued clouds, so gamesome free,
That watched with heavy binding vapor-shroud

To cast 'round stranger's steps
That dared to tread in stealth
Their realm of scenic wealth.

And I did swoon
To spy, by light of miser moon,
The deep, deep hollow hall of space below—
Dimly adorned with weirdsome light, aglow
On pictures of twinkling, sleeping cities;
Shadowy trees, leaves inert in resting breeze;
And tall soldier-stones, and valleys,
Bright in silhouette.

The moonlight dim
Did slowly, strangely change to light of dawn.
There stood the temple-observatory,
Vacant and solitary.
Alas, O Royal Phoebus!
Where were thy swarming lovers,
As blushing red thou didst burn
In earliest hour of dawn?
The test of biting chill
Drove all the votaries away,
And all was still;
I alone was left
With thee upon the hill.

Thou wert aflame,

Yet calmer art thou now,
With silvery brow,
Spreading o'er all sleeping things
Thy wakening glow.
They did awake:
The trees breathed deep;
The streamlets opened twinkling, crystal eyes—
All creation rose from sleep.
O Sun, redeemer of darkness! Now I know:
All things, all wakened creatures
Are looking in wonder
Not at thee, but at the Unseen Wonder
That through thy glow
Mutely thou wantst to show.
Where went the cold?
Rebuked, it fled, that troublesome chill of old.

I loved the breathless subtle air,
So pure and clear,
That chokes the gross
And burns the dross
Of those that love
To worship Thee in breathless state,* oh, far above
The roar and din of tipsy senses.

---

* A yogi attains the superconscious state by silencing at will
the natural tumults: thought, heartbeat, and breath. Manifesting his essential being as Spirit, he thus removes all
barriers and communes freely with Nature in any of her
myriad forms.

There on Pikes Peak
I met all minds;
I asked the winds,
Pursued the rainbow,
Begged the pure white clouds
(Which sailed unknown so proud)
To tell me if they saw
Him whom I'd just spied —
Whose One Face to see I'd tried
Midst bewitching, bewildering, diverse crowds
Of scenic faces.
And in joy I cried aloud,
"See Him hide
Beneath the beauty tide!"

OM

Another rendition of this poem appears in "Whispers from Eternity," First Version edition. A variation was set to music, and appears in "Cosmic Chants."

Whence, oh, this soundless roar doth come,
When drowseth matter's dreary drum?
The booming Om* on bliss' shore breaks;
All heaven, all earth, all body shakes.

Cords bound to flesh are broken all,
Vibrations vile do fly and fall;
The hustling heart, the boasting breath
No more disturb the yogi's health.

The house is lulled in darkness soft,
Dim, shiny light is seen aloft,
Subconscious dreams have gone to bed;
'Tis then that one doth hear Om's tread.

The bumblebee doth hum along,
Baby Om, hark! sings his song.
Krishna's flute is sounding sweet,
'Tis time the watery God to meet.

---

* An alternate transliteration of Aum, the threefold energy of creation, preservation, and destruction. Cosmic Intelligent Vibration.

God of fire is now singing,
Om! Om! his harp is ringing.
God of *prana*† is now sounding,
Wondrous bell, the soul resounding.

Upward climb the living tree,‡
Hear the sound of etheral sea;
Marching mind doth homeward hie
To join the Christmas Symphony.§

From Om, the soundless roar! From Om
The call for light o'er dark to roam.
From Om the music of the spheres.
From Om the mist of nature's tears.
All things of earth and heaven declare,
Om! Om! Resounding everywhere!

† Vibration of life energy. The five lower centers in the cerebrospinal axis control the elements in man of earth, water, fire, air, and ether. The vibratory activities of each center produce a characteristic sound. In meditation the yogi first hears the hum, as of a bumblebee, emitted by the earth *chakra* at the base of the spine. The water center has a flutelike sound, fire a harplike sound, air a bell-like sound, and ether a sound like the roar of a distant sea.

‡ The spinal cord, containing the astral centers of life and consciousness that outwardly enliven the physical body and inwardly bestow divine awakening.

§ A poetic description of the harmonious blending of all the distinctive sounds of the spinal centers with the universal, all-pervading cosmic sound of Om, heard when the mind of the meditating devotee is fixed in the medullary *chakra* and at the Christ-consciousness ("Christmas") center between the eyebrows.

THE ROYAL WAY

This ever-trodden path —
Where travelers all of earth
Do walk in joyous haste
Or slothful sorrow's state —
I walk and wonder
In truth or blunder.

The path is cleft
To right and left,
In front, behind.
Such diverse ways I find,
Conundrum enclosed, bewildered am I —
As baffling mazes do they lie.

Still, they say,
There is a royal way
For all — the right, the error-wed.
A subway path of ruby red,
Which far beneath lies hid,
For keen ones' eager eyes to spy;
It leads straight on their feet
Where all paths do meet.*

* The "royal way" refers to the subtle cerebrospinal axis of
man with its seven centers of spiritual force. On this path "all
paths do meet," for the consciousness of all seekers ultimately
follows this way of ascension to attain divine illumination.
The "subway path of ruby red" is the *muladhara* "lotus," or
basic root center whose "petals" or rays of light are red-
colored. By right meditation on God, the devotee opens the
muladhara and his consciousness then rises through the various plexuses until it reaches the highest of all, the *sahasrara* in
the brain. There the devotee attains God-realization.

NATURE'S NATURE

Away, ye muses, all away!
Away with songs of finch and fay.
Away the jaundiced sight
That magnifies the firefly's light
To bonfire bright;
That sets ablaze at once
My musing's dimly burning lamps;
That ornaments with rhymes
The penury-stricken looks betimes;
That over-clothes the logic-lord
With fancy-swollen words.
Away, the partial love
That 'boldens Nature to sit above
Her Maker!

This day I fasten eyelid doors,
With absence wax my ears,
With languorous peace congeal
My tongue, my touch, my tears,*
That I within may pore
Upon the things behind, ahead,
In the darkness round me spread.
I lock Dame Nature out
With all her fickle rout.

* Reference to the interiorization of the mind during deep
yoga meditation, in which the attention is disconnected from
sensory distractions and focused on the Spirit within.

Somewhere here,
In the darkness drear,
I myself with cheer
My course will steer
In the path
E'er sought by all:
Its magnet call
I hear.

Not here, not here,
Apollo would his burning chariot steer;
Nor Diana dare to peep
Into the sacred silence deep.

Not here, not here,
Nor far or near
Can mounts or rebel waves
E'er make me full of fear;
Nor evermore
Their dreadful grandeur to adore.

Not here, not here,
The soft capricious wiles of flowers;
Nor swarming storm clouds' sweeping terror,
Dishevelling the trees
And light-haired skies;
Nor doomsday's thunderous roar,
Dismantling earth and stars —
The cosmic beauties all to mar —

Not Nature's murderous mutiny,
Nor man's exploding destiny
Can touch me here.

Not here, not here:
Through mind's strong iron bars,
Not gods or goblins, men or nature,
Without my pass dare enter.

I look behind, ahead—
On naught but darkness tread.
In wrath I strike, and set the dark ablaze
With the immortal spark of thought,
By friction-process brought
Of concentration
And distraction.
The darkness burns
With a million tongues;
And now I spy
All past, all distant things, as nigh.

I smile serene
As I expose to gaze,
In wisdom's brilliant blaze,
All charms of the Hidden Home Unseen:
The Home of Nature's birth,
The planets' moulding hearth,
The factory whence all forms or fairies start,
The bards, colossal minds, and hearts,

123

The gods and all,
And all, and all!

Away, away
With all the lightsome lays!
Oh, now will I portray
In humble way,
And try to lisp, if only in half-truths,
Of wordless charms of Thee Unseen,
To whom Dame Nature owes her nature
    and her sheen.

AT "SUL MONTE"

*Paramahansaji dedicated this poem to Amelita Galli-Curci
and her husband, Homer Samuels, after a visit to "Sul
Monte," their home in the Catskills.*

They say that He's remote, unseen,
Austere, beyond our vision keen;
Yet, passing through the tunnel of leaves
And seeing the hilltop green —
A grassy orchid-vase,
Adorned with little doll-sized temple,
Artistic, grand, yet simple;
Hanging, it seemed, from the big skyey roof
High amidst the clouds; aloof
From din and uproars loud
Of aimless rushing crowd —
I asked myself:
Who made this? Who made that?
And found my answers
From His servitors,
Oh, everywhere, oh, everywhere!

The painted screens of varying light and shade
Did drop, go up, or fade;
The changing, charming scenic players
Did speak of Him, did entertain, and disappear.
Rows of motley costumed leaves did stand
And dance in tune with playing breeze
Or fitful thunder-band.

Turbaned soldier-trees —
Serious, majestic, grim —
Emerging from colossal mountain-castles
Stood in the distance dim
To bold declare:
"Hark, He's very close! Wake, He's very near!"
Soon with nightly curtain-fall,
They would vanish all.

By the flower-fringed lawn I was strolling
When a song came wafting, trilling.
"Is it nightingale," I thought, "or fairy voice?"
Nay, coloratura of celestial choice!
I listened — enraptured;
And when I thought the song was best,
That the voice had passed the supreme test,

126

There came whistling a deeper, deepest,
    mystic note
Straight from her soul, from the spirit remote.

Oft round the tiny temple
The listening breeze drank long
The music sweet of Homer,
And her soul-solacing song;
And in wild joy would call
The wren, the whipporwill, and all
To this peace-bathed God-altar pure,
Where man's beauty-touches rare
Have softened Nature's scenic paintings bare.

Midst all the august guests,
A few forget-me-nots
(From unknown somewhere)
Came peeping through the temple door.
"To remind us," said Ameli,
"'Love not My creations more than Me.'"

Dear Homer, Amelita,
Through little forget-me-nots
Thy Father will speak to thee ever and ever:
"Forget Me not, oh, never, never!
Amelita of 'Sul Monte' and Homer,
Remember Me ever, ever."

THE TOILER'S LAY

From school of life,
From bossy duty's binding day,
From hours of dollar-strife,
I wish I were a runaway!

From harrying worry-hound
I'll flee one day.
From crowds and restless throngs around
I wish I were a runaway!

From greedy food
That inside steals its way,
From luring dainties' tempting mood,
I wish I were a runaway!

From homely chairs and banal couch
The call of grassy bed today
My heart's desire doth snatch.
I wish I were a runaway!

Someday, from Nature-given cup —
My hollowed hands — I'll drink
At streamlet's bounteous brink.
With finger-forks I'll eat the meat
Of fresh-plucked fruits; my seat
All snug beneath the shady trees
Enlivened by songs of birds and bumblebees,

And fanned by mothering air.

From care and tear
I'll bathe my weary mind
In joyous new-made day.
Away dishwashing, cups and saucers — all away!
    For just a day
I wish I were a runaway!

MOHAWK TRAIL

Welcomed by a fresh and smiling day,
Ushered by trees benign that overlay,
Shading our bodies from the jealous sun;
With wheels of rubber pressing asphalt road,
And softly humming motor-noise we rode
The Mohawk Trail where Adam lies.*

Unlike some other joyful rides
When mind, with sameness dulled, did oft abide
The time and common scenes in passive mood,
My mind was full and bright and good.
A strange unknown, unthought, new thrill,
Did o'er me steal in soothing sweep so still.
I raced the wind, and scattered smiles
That played with sunshine, spread for miles.

My secret-hoarded joy in vault of soul
Extravagantly did I spend withal,
To purchase Nature's e're new gaudy scenes
Shown by hasty, racing peddler windshield screen.
My spirit, too long hemmed in city's narrow walls,
Once more was free; all nature sent a joyous call—
The waving leaves of trees, the babbling rill,
Impatient wind, the smiling sky, and patient hill.

---

* North Adams (Massachusetts), a town at the end of the
Mohawk Trail. In a play on this name, Paramahansaji alludes
indirectly to the beautiful countryside, like the Eden enjoyed
by the primal Adam.

WHISPERS

The leaves do sigh;
They cannot speak
Of the One on high.
The birds do sing;
They cannot say
What in their bosoms springs.
The beasts do howl
With muffled soul;
They never can say nigh
What in their feelings lies.
Since I can sing or say or cry,
Mightily will I try
To pour out whispers Thine — all and each —
That to hearts do softly reach.

LISTEN TO MY SOUL SONG

The stanza next to the last was set to music by Paramahansaji for his "Cosmic Chants."

Come! Listen to my soul-song!

The darkness burst,
And Thy descending shafts of light
Pierced the heart of gloom
To listen to my soul song.

Though hidden Thou art
Behind the screen of my eyes,
Thou dost remain, unseen,
To listen to my soul song.

Burst the veils! Burst the blue!
Burst all lights!
And come to me as Thou art,
To listen to my soul song.

Burst my senses and my mind!
Burst my heart and feeling!
Burst my silence and my soul
To listen to my soul song.

In the breeze I feel Thy touch;
In the sun, Thy warm love.
In the colorful scenery, I behold Thy beauty-face;

In the waves, I see Thee dancing — ever dancing!
And Thou art dancing o'er my thoughts
To listen to my soul song.

Listen to my soul song!
Burst the heart, burst the sky, burst the soul!
Come, listen to my soul song!
Hovering over the clouds,
Lingering over the lea —
Thou hast come
To listen to my soul song.

Beneath the gloaming
Of dim devotion of eyes unseeing,
Hidden Thou dost remain —
To listen to my soul song.

LIFE'S DREAM

Dedicated to the Self-Realization Fellowship Headquarters on Mount Washington in Los Angeles, California, established by Paramahansa Yogananda in October 1925

The summery East
And the wintry West,
They say;
But Mount Washington
(Named rightly after that pioneer
Of freedom's great career),
Thou dost stand, a snowless guardian Himalaya
Of the Angel Land,* in perpetual green regalia.

Nippon's camphor trees; perfumed wisteria,
    smiling roses;
Palm and date; and well-remembered spicy bay leaf
    trees of Hind stand close

* Los Angeles. Its full name was originally Ciudad de Los Angeles, "City of the Angels."

With endless scenic beauties —
Of ocean, canyon, setting sun, moon-studded sky,
And nightly twinkling cities —
To declare Thine ever-changing beauty.

Mount Washington! Thy crown shall newly wear
A priceless starry jewel — a school of life —
Which, for all future, here
Shall draw lost travelers from East and West,
To find their Goal, their own One Place of rest.

Here all other paths shall merge as one.
Here love of earthly freedom's paradise, America,
Shall blend fore'er with love of spiritual freedom's
    paradise, India.
Here church in deepest friendliness shall other
    churches meet,
And temple, too, the mosque shall greet.
Here long divorcèd matter-laws
Shall wed again in peace the Spirit-laws.
Here all minds can learn the true art
Of living life; the way to start
Straight toward the one great Place
Where all must meet at last.
Jehovah! This is the land of solace
Where my life's dream in truth reappears!*

---

* Readers of Paramahansaji's *Autobiography of a Yogi* may
recall that long before he came to America, he had had
visions of Mt. Washington: at his Guru's hermitage in Seram-
pore, and later, on a trip with Sri Yukteswar, in Kashmir.

THY SECRET THRONE

Behind the screen
Of all things seen,
How dost Thou hide—
Elude the tide
Of marching human eyes,
That 'round Thee rushing hies?
'Twill not be long
Ere will be known
Thy hiding place,
By children with Thine eyes and grace.

Sage science splits
Each atom knit
By Thee, to find apace
Thy hiding place.
Is heart of atom, electron,
Thy secret throne?
Deep we bore
To find Thine art and lore
Of doings all sublime,
Hidden betimes.
Yet Thine abode
Seems far, remote;
'Tis still to find
With deeper mind.

THY CRUEL SILENCE

I prayed to Thee,
But Thou wert mute.
At Thy door I knocked;
Thou answered not.
I gave my tears
To soft'n Thy heart;
In cruel silence
Didst Thou watch.
But now I've learned
The way to earn
Attention Thine:
I'll weep and pray
Unceasingly —
In cruel silence, if need be —
Till time is old,
And earth grows cold;
Till life doth fail,
Till body fall.
Then if Thou speakest,
And dost wish me peace,
Still will I pray and weep —
In cruel silence deep.

ETERNITY

Oh, will that day arrive
When I shall ceaselessly ask — yea, drive
Eternal questions into Thine ear,
O Eternity! and have solution
How weak weeds grow and stand unbent,
Unshaken 'neath the trampling current.
How the storm wrecks titanic things;
Uproots the trees,
And quick disturbs the mighty seas.
How the first spark blinked; how the first tree,
The first goldfish, the first bluebird so free,
And the first crooning baby,
Into this wonder-house to visit,
Made their grand entry.
They come, I see;
Their growth alone I watch.

Thy cosmic moulding Hand,
That secret works on land and sea,
I wish to seize,
O Eternity!

THE HART OF HEAVEN

Inspired by Francis Thompson's "The Hound of Heaven"

Like a wild, cruel hunter,
Sure of my prey,
I chased the Heavenly Hart
Through forests of dark desires,
Mazes of passing pleasures.
Down corridors of ignorance
I raced for Him — the Hart of Heaven.

Farther, farther He fled,
Driven by fear of me
Equipped with spears of selfishness.

And earth echoed, as He fled:
    "I am more fleet,
    Swifter than thy feet,
    Thy fiery passion's greed
    That vainly rushes at Me.
    None capture Me
    Who Me affright
    And thus make wise."

Pursuing the Deer,
I flew the heavenly plane of prayer;
But crashed to earth —
By restlessness felled.

The Deer yet fled,
And Its echoing voice said:
    "Fleeter am I
    Than the noisy plane of prayer.
    Thy loud-tongued hollow words
    But startled me
    In the earliest hour of the chase.
    Beyond thy sight I race!"

My spears, my hunting dogs, my plane I left;
Stealthily I crept,
Holding firm my dart of concentration —
All sudden, lo!
I spied the Hart of Heaven grazing peacefully,
Fearless before me.
I swift took aim and shot,
But my hand with unsteadiness shook.
The Deer bounded;
And earth resounded:
    "Without devotion,
    Thou art a poor, poor marksman!"

Again and yet again I shot
At the Heavenly Hart,
But easily It fled, with echoing cry:
    "Beyond the range of mental dart —
    O far beyond — am I!"

In despair, I gave up the chase:

Then, led by intuition strange, and curious
    wondering,
I found a secret lair of love in me,
And strollèd deep within.
There came my Hart of Heaven — lo!
Willingly entering in.

Eager, devoted, steadily
I shot again, again,
With concentration-dart;
Afraid the Deer might flee anew.
Ofttimes I missed; yet It stirred not,
Moved not, fled not.
Finally, my Heavenly Hart,
Now wounded by devotion's dart,
Lay gasping, dying, in me.

Its vanishing breath —
Singing throughout the silent earth —
Echoed within me:
    "None can seize Me
    Save with help of Mine,
    Save only Mine!
    I am thine! Receive Me!"

THE GRAND CANYON
OF THE COLORADO

Who reigns in this canyon,
Deep and grand with measureless space —
The sun or moon?
They jealously vie
To drive away with swiftness
The demon of darkness,
And try to wake the sleeping motley splendor
That decorates in glory
The crowded temple-peaks, both young and hoary.

These shrines, though different, yet in unison
Do welcome all to see the One;
E'en as the temples of Shiva and Rama
In silence worship the one Brahma.*

Who reigns here?
The One — with different shapes and names
To inspire
All eyes, all minds, all sects, all creeds,
As suits their wide aesthetic needs;
And cause them to bow in awe and reverence
To the Spirit of Vastness
That here reigns.

* Three towering peaks (about 8,000 ft.), so named in 1882
by Clarence Dutton of the U.S. Geological Survey because of
their resemblance to Hindu temples.

THE HARVEST

Drawn by joy sublime,
I watch each harvest time,
When furrowed sky glows red with ripe sunbeams;
But never have I found Thy ploughing teams.
The oriole's glowing painted breast is shown,
And yet Thy brush, O Painter, ne'er is known!
The North Star timely leaps,
Nocturnal watch unfailing keeps;
Thy house the sun and seasons supervise,
Yet Thou, O Master, seemest not to rise!

LEAVE THY VOW OF SILENCE

Blossoms come and seasons change;
They all speak of Thee.
The moon slightly shows Thy smile;
The sun holds Thy lamp of life.
In the arteries of leaves
I see Thy blood flowing.
In every thought of mine
Thy heart is beating loud.
Throw off Thy shroud of nature —
Wake from Thy sleep, O Lord.

I have been swimming for Thee
In the sea of my tears.
When wilt Thou talk to me,
Leaving Thy vow of silence?
Wake! Wake! from Thy sleep —
Speak to me now, O Lord.

MYSTERY

Burst, inky cloud, do burst;
Fling open thy fathomless gloom!
In thy dark chamber must
A million mysteries loom.

Heartless, staring sky!
Make quick reply
To aching query of my straining eye;
Show what thou hidest, and why.

The ceaseless surging thoughts
Go mocking, dancing by,
I long to know their lot.

Someone did throw me free
To battle all alone in this rough sea.
Rudderless I drift; stranded on shoals,
My boat I could not shift.

I'll burst the clouds, I'll clear the shoals;
I'll rip the sky in twain,
I'll break my heart,
With questions crush my brain.
I'll ask and pray,
Will beg or steal,
To find the friends long stolen away —
To know their woe or weal.

This wondrous day,
Stage set for play
By Unseen Hand;
The players drop
From no-man's land,
Then vanish all away.
With changing scenes of birth and death,
    The drama's on.
    The actors play anon,
    Yet know not why they play
This glorious day.

OCEANIC PRESENCE

As I sailed away from You on the river of desire,
Suddenly I found myself launched on Your
    oceanic presence.
Though I ran away from You through the fog
    of incarnations,
I arrived at the threshold of Your all-pervading
    temple.
In the sphere of thought I flew—
North, south, east, west;
But the net of Your omnipresence surrounded me.
Riding the wings of swiftest electrons,
I dived below, into the bowels of eternity,
Only to find You there.
Above, into eternity's heart I zoomed;
But no matter how far I went,
You stood always ahead of me.
In desperation, unable to flee from You,
I plunged to the east, to the west, in eternity's
    chasms,
And there I fell in Your lap.
At last, with the dynamite of my will,
I exploded the airship of my self, my thoughts,
    my love,
Into countless dust specks of fading life,
Floating everywhere, into all things—
And found that I slept in Your bosom.

Because I kept my own eyes closed,
I thought I was hiding from You;
But before Your watchful eyes, ever-present am I.
Open my eyes that I may behold You,
Looking at me from all sides, everywhere.
For though I may try to hide from You,
    and think I do;
Wherever I am, there are You.

FLIGHT!

An experience in samadhi

I closed my eyes and saw the skies
Of dim opalescent infinity spread round me.
The grey sky-chariot of the dawn of awakening,
Displaying searchlight eyes,
Came and took me away.
I zoomed through space,
Boring through the ether of mystery.
I passed through age-hidden spiral nebulae.
Willy-nilly I went on and on,
Left, right, north, south, above and below.
I found no landing.
I went through many tailspins of distractions,
But I spun through limitlessness.
I whirled through an eternal furnace of lights.
At last, bit by bit, my plane melted
In that transmuting flame;
And then, bit by bit, my body melted
In that purifying fire.
Bit by bit my thoughts melted—
My feelings became pure liquid light.

IN THE LAND OF DREAMS

Each night, as my spirit roams
In spheres of slumber vast,
I become a hermit and renounce
My title, body-form, possessions, creeds—
Breaking the self-erected prison walls
Of flesh and earthly limitations.
I am an all-pervading Son of God,
No longer caged in brittle, dingy clod;
Nor tied by tangible cords of birth,
Or man-made smallness, social standing,
And duty-shadows of earth.

There in sleepland's ether eternal,
I have no country, no homeland dear;
Nor am I Hindu or Christian seer;
Nor Occidental nor Oriental,
Race-bound behind the bars of inheritance.
In dreamland's limitless acres,
My spirit revels in freedom—
Its only religion freedom—
Gypsying gaily there,
Pilfering joy from everywhere
No lordling god o'ershadows me—
None but Myself to rule myself.
Behold, the slave-man hath become the god!
The sleeping mortal, the awakened deathless Lord!

An unseen, unheard god am I,
Drinking, breathing gladness;
Gliding in wingèd glory
Through the endless land!
Free from haunting fears,
Or possible crash and shattered skull:
No solids there to give me hurt,
No liquids to drown me deep;
No vile, dank vapors to choke me,
No fire my unseen form to burn.
Free from the memory, e'en,
Of a fragile body-dream,

O'er infinite space am I spread.
All things am I!
How, then, could aught
Dare injure me?
The heart of the big Myself
Would break
If it should strike
The little myself.

Unknown to others, but known to Myself,
I wake and walk and dream,
Eat and drink and glide in Joy.
I Myself am the Joy I sought —
The Joy that all do seek.
So little, ah, so finite, I,
When I dreamt in my sleepy wakefulness.
Boundless big am I, awake
In my sleepless wakefulness!

AT THE ROOTS OF ETERNITY

With sailing clouds and plunging breeze,
With singing leaves and youthful storms,
   capricious seas,
With bounding planet-balls — all these —
Absorbed, I wildly play,
Forgetful of Thee; but not alway.
At close of day
My eager hands I lay
At Thy hidden roots,
    O Eternity,
To seize the nectar-loot
That when tapped flows free.

THE SPELL

Ah, this old, old nectar of night,
Brewed below by sun-god bright —
Let every little fleshly cell
That's tired and thirsty drink it well;
By soothing spell of sleep eject
All aches that heart and brain infect.

That spell, quick marching on,
Falls o'er me now, so warm,
And robs my mind
Of linkèd thoughts, to bind
Me prisoner in its charm.

A MIRROR NEW

I bring to you
A mirror new—
A glass of introspection clear,
That illusion shows, and sooty fear
That spots thy mind.

Thou wilt also find
This mirror new
  Would loyal show, all true,
  The "Inner You"
That's veiled in flesh
And never doth appear.

Each night consult afresh thy mirror-friend;
And ere the sorcerer Sleep doth call,
Make use to see thyself withal—
And clear away
Dust of that day.

EVASION

Whene'er I almost see Thee,
Thou dost vanish suddenly.
When Thou art nearly trapped in me,
I look, and find Thee gone.
E'en when I think I've seized Thee,
Thou dost e'er escape.
How long this hide-and-seek and play?
I'm weary with the toil of day.
Still, I may brook this game — evasion Thine —
If 'tis for but a tiny flash of time;
That in the end I clear may see
Thy face! with doubled joy and mind that's free.

METHOUGHT I HEARD A VOICE

While singing by the rill
My voice did softly thrill
With echoes of my thought
By fancies brought.

I wandered in my play
On faerie field away;
And stopped to muse, rejoice —
Methought I heard a Voice!

The flowers of that field,
Of wondrous hues, perfumed
With essence of the heart, did yield
Delicious joys undreamed.

Behind the thin bright veiling
Of blossom-scented feelings,
I saw a fitful flash —
Some Glistening Presence rush!

I tiptoe stood,
Listening, watching;
I poured my heart,
Listening, watching.

I AM HERE

Alone I roamed by the ocean's shore,
And watched
     The wrestling waves in brawling roar—
Alive with Thine own restless life,
Thine angry mood in ripply quiver—
Until Thy wrathful vastness made me shiver
And turn away from nature's heated strife.
And then
     A kindly, spreading sentinel tree
Waved friendly arms to comfort me—
Consoling me with gentler look sublime,
Its swaying leaves in tender lullaby-rhyme,
Singing a message that I knew was Thine.
Above
     I saw the gaugeless, mystic sky;
And, childlike, in the valley dim I sought to pry
At Thee, and to play with Thee.
But in vain I sought Thy body, hiding there,
Cloud-robed, foam-sprayed, leaf-garlanded—
Too rare for mortal eyes to see, or ears to hear.
And yet,
     I knew that Thou wert always near,
As if to play at hide-and-seek with me,
Receding when I almost touched Thee,
Groping to find Thee through the maddening fold
Of ignorance dark—old as time is old.
At last,

I ceased my search in dim despair,
My search for Thee! O Thou Royal Sly Eluder!
   . . . everywhere,
Yet seeming nowhere . . . lost in unplumbed space,
Where none may clasp Thee or behold Thy face!
In haste,
     I ceased my fruitless seach and hied *away* from
     Thee!
Still, still no answer from the wrathful sea,
And only whispers from the friendly tree;
Just silence from the limitless blue sky—
Silence from valley low and mountain high!
Like a hurt child, *within the depths of me*
I hid and sulked — no longer seeking Thee.
When lo!
     Unheralded, some Unseen Hand
Suddenly snatched away the all-black band
That had so blinded me with fold on fold.
No longer weary, filled with strength untold,
I stood, and watched again
A laughing sea, instead of wrathful roars,
A gay, glad world, with mystically opened doors.
With only mists of dreams between,
Someone beside me stood unseen—
And whispered to me, cool and clear:
     "Hello, playmate! I am here!"

MY PRISONER

Long didst Thou hide
Beneath the static of my restless thoughts;
Long didst Thou flee
In the chambers of eerie ether.

At last I hunted Thee down
In quiet desert-dunes
Of my desirelessness.

Fastened with strong cords of devotion,
Thou art my Prisoner.

I'll lock Thee
In the cell of silence,
Secure behind bars of my closed eyes.

Within the temple of my dreams,
Beloved Captive,
I'll hide Thee
In a bower of caresses.

Precious Prisoner,
I'll enshrine Thee
On the altar of my secret songs.

Infinite Personage,
I'll cloister Thee
Behind strong walls of my undying love.

I AM LONELY NO MORE

I am not lonely in the chamber of solitude,
For Thou art always there.
I am lonely amidst an uproarious crowd,
In which Thy silence slips away
Like a startled, fast-footed, large-eyed deer.
When I had found Thee not,
I was lonely in a crowd of thoughts
And solitary in the chamber of myself, thinking:
"Alone I came from the unknown
And alone I must depart into the unknown."
Finding Thee, I have learned
To make mine own Thee alone,
On the lonely wayside of life
Or on its crowded thoroughfare.
For now I behold the unseen links
In front of and behind this life,
Hidden in post-mortem and prenatal chambers.
From my Known-One I came,
In my Known-One I live,
In my Known-One finally I'll dive.

Away from Myself I was lonely —
But since my little self met the big Self,
I am lonely no more.

SOME TREASURE OF MY OWN

Whatever I sought to give You
I found was Yours.
So I took away the flowers from the altar,
And snuffed out the candles in the temple,
For I would offer You some treasure of my own.

Searching on the tract of my heart, lo!
Rare perennial plants I found,
Of innate craving for You.
You are mine — what joy!
And 'tis my free choice to love You as mine.

Though love came from You,
And was Your gift to me,
That love is Yours no longer,
Because You gave it to me.
With this love You have given,
Belonging now to me alone,
I want to love You.

Your gift of love, I know,
Is unconditioned by command to love You only —
I could have used Your love forever
To worship just Your gifts,
Or to become saturated with the desires
Of a material life.

But I will only pick flowers of love
From those undying plants of my soul-craving—
Blooming amidst the garden of incarnations—
And lay them in the temple of Your heart;
For these alone are mine.

Of my own accord I love You;
Through my own desire, I prefer You to Your gifts;
And I use my free choice
To offer all my love to You alone — naught else.
You must receive what's mine: the love I freely give,
Sole treasure of my own.

THEY ARE THINE

I have nothing to offer Thee,
For all things are Thine.
I grieve not that I cannot give;
For nothing is mine, for nothing is mine.
Here I lay at Thy feet
My life, my limbs, my thoughts and speech;
For they are Thine, for they are Thine.

WHEN I CAST ALL DREAMS AWAY

I sipped the sap of each sane pleasure;
I exulted in the crushed beauty of sextillion stars;
I made a bonfire of all sorrows and basked in the
    glory blaze;
I quaffed the questing love of all hearts;
I mingled paternal, maternal, and fraternal love
    together,
And drank the solacing draught;
I squeezed the scriptures for drops of peace;
I wrung poems from the winepress of Nature;
I lifted gems from the mine of thoughts;
I stole the sweetness from the honeycomb
    of innocent joys;
I read, I smiled, I worked, I planned, I throbbed, I
    aspired;
      But naught was sufficient.
Only nightmares of incompleteness,
Ever receding will-o'-the-wisps of promised
    happiness,
Haunted and hastened my heart.
      But when I cast all dreams away,
      I found the deep sanctuary of peace,
      And my soul sang: "God alone! God alone!"

MY NATIVE LAND

The friendly sky,
Inviting shade of banyan tree,
The holy Ganges flowing by —
How can I forget thee!

I love the waving corn
Of India's fields so bright,
Oh, better than those heav'nly grown
By deathless gods of might!

My soul's broad love, by God's command,
Was first born here below,
In my own native land —
On India's sunny soil aglow.

I love thy breeze,
I love thy moon,
I love thy hills and seas;
In thee I wish my life to cease.

Thou taught'st me first to love
The sky, the stars, the God above;
So my first homage — as 'tis meet —
I lay, O India, at thy feet!

From thee I now have learned to see,
To love all lands alike as thee.
I bow to thee, my native land,
Thou mother of my love so grand.

MY INDIA

Not where the musk of happiness blows,
Nor where darkness and fears never tread;
Not in the homes of perpetual smiles,
Nor in the heaven of a land of prosperity
Would I be born,
If I must put on mortal garb once more.

Dread famine may prowl and tear my flesh,
Yet would I love to be again
In my Hindustan.
A million thieves of disease
May try to steal the body's fleeting health;
And clouds of fate
May shower scalding drops of searing sorrow—
Yet would I there, in India,
Love to reappear!

Is this love of mine blind sentiment
That sees not the pathways of reason?
Ah, no! I love India,
For there I learned first to love God
    and all things beautiful.
Some teach to seize the fickle dewdrop, life,
Sliding down the lotus leaf of time;
Stubborn hopes are built
Around the gilded, brittle body-bubble.
But India taught me to love

The soul of deathless beauty in the dewdrop
    and the bubble—
Not their fragile frames.
Her sages taught me to find my Self,
Buried beneath the ash heaps
Of incarnations of ignorance.
Through many a land of power, plenty, and science
My soul, garbed sometimes as an Oriental,
Sometimes as an Occidental,
Traveled far and wide,
Seeking Itself;
At last, in India, to find Itself.

Though mortal fires raze all her homes
    and golden paddy fields,
Yet to sleep on her ashes and dream immortality,
O India, I will be there!
The guns of science and matter
Have boomed on her shores,
Yet she is unconquered.
Her soul is free evermore!
Her soldier saints are away,
To rout with realization's ray
The bandits of hate, prejudice, and
    patriotic selfishness;
And to burn the walls of separation dark
Between children of the One, One Father.
The Western brothers by matter's might
    have conquered my land;

Blow, blow aloud, her conch shells all!
India now invades with love,
To conquer their souls.

Better than Heaven or Arcadia
I love Thee, O my India!
And thy love I shall give
To every brother nation that lives.
God made the earth;
Man made confining countries
And their fancy-frozen boundaries.
But with newfound boundless love
I behold the borderland of my India
Expanding into the world.
Hail, mother of religions, lotus, scenic beauty,
    and sages!
Thy wide doors are open,
Welcoming God's true sons through all ages.
Where Ganges, woods, Himalayan caves, and
    men dream God—
I am hallowed; my body touched that sod.

GOD! GOD! GOD!

From the depths of slumber,
As I ascend the spiral stairway of wakefulness,
I whisper:
God! God! God!

Thou art the food, and when I break my fast
Of nightly separation from Thee,
I taste Thee, and mentally say:
God! God! God!

No matter where I go, the spotlight of my mind
Ever keeps turning on Thee;
And in the battle din of activity my silent war-cry
    is ever:
God! God! God!

When boisterous storms of trials shriek
And worries howl at me,
I drown their noises, loudly chanting:
God! God! God!

When my mind weaves dreams
With threads of memories,
On that magic cloth I do emboss:
God! God! God!

Every night, in time of deepest sleep,
My peace dreams and calls: Joy! Joy! Joy!
And my joy comes singing evermore:
God! God! God!

In waking, eating, working, dreaming, sleeping,
Serving, meditating, chanting, divinely loving,
My soul constantly hums, unheard by any:
God! God! God!

GOD'S BOATMAN

I want to ply my boat, many times,
Across the gulf-after-death,
And return to earth's shores
From my home in heaven.

174

I want to load my boat
With those waiting, thirsty ones
Who are left behind,
And carry them by the opal pool
Of iridescent joy
Where my Father distributes
His all-desire-quenching liquid peace.

Oh, I will come again and again!
Crossing a million crags of suffering,
With bleeding feet, I will come —
If need be, a trillion times —
So long as I know
One stray brother is left behind.

I want Thee, O God,
That I may give Thee to all.
I want salvation,
That I may give it to all.
Free me, then, O God,
From the bondage of the body,
That I may show others
How they can free themselves.
I want Thine everlasting bliss
Only that I may share it with others;
That I may show all my brothers
The way to happiness
Forever and forever, in Thee.

WHEN I AM ONLY A DREAM

I come to tell you all of Him,
And the way to encase Him in your bosom,
And of the discipline that brings His grace.
Those of you who have asked me
To guide you to my Beloved's presence—
I warn you through my silently talking mind,
Or speak to you through a gentle significant glance,
Or whisper to you through my love,
Or loudly dissuade you when you stray away
    from Him.

But when I shall become only a memory, or a
    mental image, or silently speaking voice,
When no earthly call will ever reveal
My whereabouts in unplumbed space,
When no shallow entreaty or stern stentorian
    command will bring from me an answer—
I will smile in your mind when you are right,
And when you are wrong I will weep through
    my eyes,
Dimly peering at you in the dark,
And weep through your eyes, perchance;
And I will whisper to you through your conscience,
And I will reason with you through your reason,
And I will love all through your love.
When you are able no longer to talk with me,
Read my *Whispers from Eternity;*

Eternally through it I will talk to you.
Unknown I will walk by your side
And guard you with invisible arms.
And as soon as you know my Beloved
And hear His voice in silence,
You will know me again more tangibly
    than you knew me on this earth plane.
And yet when I am only a dream to you,
I will come to remind you that you too are naught
But a dream of my Heavenly Beloved;
And when you know you are a dream,
    as I know now,
We will be ever awake in Him.

THE DYING YOUTH'S DIVINE REPLY

Paramahansaji here describes a vision in which "God showed me the right attitude man should have toward death."

In his laughter he had often heard
The echo of God's merriment.
This laughing youth of many charms
Lay dying in a hamlet,
Yet the blast of illness was unable to wither
    his smiles.
The doleful doctors came and said, "But a day,
But a day we give you to live."
The dear ones of his family cried aloud:
"Leave us not, poor youth of our hearts!
Our souls are bursting with pity for thee, for thy
    plight."

The smiles of the youth grew brighter,
And he joyously spoke, in a voice that sang:
"Ah, just a day; yea, but a day
Between me and my long-lost Beloved.
Oh, the hours of the day are slow to die!
But when they have all expired,
My Beloved will open the prison gates of my life
And embrace me in Her infinite arms.*

---

* In India, God is worshiped as the Divine Father, Mother, Friend, Beloved; for God is Love, the one Source of all noble forms of human love.

The balloon of life will break,
Releasing the imprisoned breath.
I'll flee the mortal shore
And reach my immaculate kingdom of dainty
    dreams,
Where no nightmares of illness will dare
To cross the threshold of my peace.

"I am a billow of the sea; in the sea I will be free.
I am a dust of light; I will swim in the stars.
I am a drop of ambrosia; I will be a sea of nectar.
I am the river of moonlight; I will melt in
    iridescence.
My nightmares of desires have ceased,
My dreams of grief are broken
By the awakening light of laughter.
The lamp of many lives, flickering over my
    earthliness,
Is extinguished forever.
My light has plunged into His Light
And is playing over the splendors of eternity.
The shadows of fanciful fears have slipped away
And His Light has spread over the dark nooks
    of my soul.

"I am making preparations with laughter and songs.
I have clothed all my thoughts with new robes.
I have asked my reverent feelings to sing a celestial
    chorus,

And I have roused all the folk living in the villa of
    inspiration
To observe this gala day for me —
The day of my entry into the Infinite Kingdom
As a son of the King of Peace.
I have asked the sentries of my will and
    determination
To banish all sad inhabitants from my kingdom,
And to kill at sight the Satan of fear, pain, sorrow,
    and attachment.
My celebration of entering the Bliss Kingdom
Must be attended only by laughter and songs;
No timidity or dark sorrow will be allowed
To join my festivity.
All the subjects of my mortal kingdom
Are roused today
To continuous, unleashed, watchful merriment:
They are waiting to welcome the divine messenger,
Delightful Death,
When he comes to open the latch of finitude
And let them in —
Into the free kingdom of Infinity.

"All the inmates of my consciousness
Are rejoicing to leave this mortal prison,
Where they have been lashed with worries,
Thrown into the dungeon of uncertain, unsafe
    living,
And pounded constantly by accidents, failures,

disease, and unhappiness.
They are glad to dump the broken cage
    of brittle bones,
To throw the prison-flesh into the fire of Infinity,
And set free the Bird of Paradise
To soar the skies of Blissful Omnipresence.
The inmates of my life are aquiver,
Waiting joyously for the slow hours to pass by,
In order to welcome savior Death when he shall
    come,
Of his own sweet accord,
And at his sovereign command
Bid them enter into his kingdom.

"Oh, dear ones, rejoice in my joy
On the eve of my freedom from the mortal prison,
Long before you.
For me, no breaking of bones, no accidents,
No fear of failure or financial loss
Will ever exist;
No cares of unpaid bills will ever keep sawing
    through my mind,
No greed for possessions will ever be gnawing
    at my soul.
No discourtesies, naggings, quarrels,
No pain or disease
Will dare intrude their noise
When the doors of all my senses are closed;
For I will be beyond their reach,

Out roaming with my Beloved
On the tracts of cosmic freedom.
Pray do not wish me back in your prison
Just to join helplessly in your chorus of wails;
But if needed,
I will gladly come a million times,
Wearing the robes of immortality,
To take you out of your mortal prison
To my Home of blessed freedom.

"I am free! Soon I will be out,
But I'll indeed be sad to look at you
Through your prison bars of mortal life,
Locked up in your misery-making mundane cell.
Don't cry for me,
Ye who are left on this desolate shore,
Still to mourn and deplore;
It is I who pity you.
'Tis now less than a day,
As the doctors say,
Till I will be on my infinite way.
No music is sweeter than this song
I am singing every moment:
'Now less than a day! less than a day,
For today my Beloved comes in the dazzling chariot
    of death
To take me away — to take me away
To the Kingdom of Deathlessness,
To the Palace of Bliss-Dreams,

Far, far away.'

"You weep for me dark tears,
Crying for your loss in me;
But I weep for you joyous tears,
Because I am going before you, for your welfare's
    sake,
To light candles of wisdom all the way;
And I shall wait to welcome you there
Where I shall be,
With my only Beloved and yours."

WHEN I TAKE THE VOW OF SILENCE

When I take the vow of silence
To remain enlocked with my Beloved
In the arms of His everywhereness,
I shall be busy listening to His symphony
Of creation's bliss songs, and beholding hidden
   wondrous visions.
Yet I shall not be oblivious of you all.
I shall mutely watch you
Walking o'er me in the fresh grass-blades
And seeing me in my living leafy presences.
I shall behold you with mothering tenderness
Through every crimson blossom
That wears a blush of love to bring you delight.
I shall caress you with the enfolding breeze
To relieve your worries and fears;
And enwrap you in sun warmth
When the chill of delusive loneliness strays
   into your heart.
When you gaze at the ocean
You will be looking right at me,
United with my Beloved on the altar of the horizon,
Sky-canopied with silver rays o'er the azure
   wavy hazy sanctuary.
I shall not speak except through your reason,
Nor scold except through your conscience.
I shall persuade only through your love
And your heart's longing to seek the Beloved only.
I shall tempt you — but with the sole temptation
To enjoy the Beloved's love alone.
Forget me if you will, but not my Beloved!
Remembering Him, you cannot forget me.